Teacher Inquiry in Literacy Workshops

NCTE Editorial Board

Teacher Inquiry in Literacy Workshops

Forging Relationships through Reggio-Inspired Practice

Edited by
Judith T. Lysaker
Purdue University

Foreword by Louise Boyd Cadwell

NCTE NATIONAL COUNCIL OF TEACHERS OF ENGLISH
1111 W. KENYON ROAD, URBANA, ILLINOIS 61801-1096

With immeasurable gratitude we dedicate
this book to the children who have taught us so very much,
to the families and friends who have supported our work, to the
administrators who have given us the flexibility to pursue our
ideas, and to Ena Shelley, who introduced us to the schools of
Reggio Emilia.

Staff Editor: Bonny Graham
Interior Design: Jenny Jensen Greenleaf
Cover Design: Pat Mayer

NCTE Stock Number: 54878

©2013 by the National Council of Teachers of English.

It is the policy of NCTE in its journals and other publications to provide a forum for the open discussion of ideas concerning the content and the teaching of English and the language arts. Publicity accorded to any particular point of view does not imply endorsement by the Executive Committee, the Board of Directors, or the membership at large, except in announcements of policy, where such endorsement is clearly specified.

Every effort has been made to provide current URLs and email addresses, but because of the rapidly changing nature of the Web, some sites and addresses may no longer be accessible.

Library of Congress Cataloging-in-Publication Data

Teacher inquiry in literacy workshops : forging relationships through Reggio-inspired practice / edited by Judith T. Lysaker, Purdue University.
    pages cm
  Includes bibliographical references and index.
  ISBN 978-0-8141-5487-8 (pbk.)
  1. Language arts (Elementary) 2. Reading (Elementary) 3. Language arts—Research.
4. Reading—Research. 5. Reggio Emilia approach (Early childhood education)
6. Critical pedagogy. I. Lysaker, Judith T.
  LB1576.T366 2013
  372.6'049—dc23
                                                                              2013006382

Contents

Foreword

One of the most intriguing concepts to me these days is the idea of an "ecotone," the zone where two habitats come together. Biologists and ecologists call what happens in this boundary area between two ecosystems the "edge effect." The edge effect produces a great diversity of species and unexpected relationships not found elsewhere. It is interesting to note that in the arts and across disciplines, two or more diverse elements bumping up against each other are among the conditions that spark creativity and innovation. *Teacher Inquiry in Literacy Workshops: Forging Relationships through Reggio-Inspired Practice* is a book about a learning ecotone, the rich and provocative zone between two educational approaches.

In this educational ecotone, Judith Lysaker and her colleagues were looking for opportunities for more meaningful teacher and student learning to emerge through their commitment to study the relationship between the theory and the practice of literacy workshops and of the Reggio approach to early childhood education.

To orient us to their shared study, Judith Lysaker opens with an introduction that explains the structure and process of the study group, followed by a chapter that outlines the principles and practices of each approach. The next six chapters tell real stories from real classrooms based on the teacher research that each participant engaged in during the year of their study. After each of these chapters, Judith leads a conversation to probe deeper into one of the aspects of each teacher's story. She concludes the book with a reflective chapter on their pedagogical experiment.

The pedagogical experiment is clear at the outset and the reader is eager to see what will unfold. It is a privilege to enter into these teachers' classrooms and learn from their journeys as they strive to deepen and enrich literacy learning for their students. The narrative voice of each teacher in this group brings the stories alive and transports the reader right into the middle of the daily life of these classrooms.

This book is based on the practice of research and the richness of relationships, two elements that are critical to both the Reggio approach and literacy workshops. The vision of this shared study was to cross-pollinate these elements and thereby lift up the quality of the teaching and learning of all the teachers and children.

To engage in successful teacher research, it is necessary to be curious, to have a focus, and to collect data. Each of the teacher-authors developed her own burning question and her own strategies for collecting anecdotal notes, children's conversations and actions, photographs of children's processes, and children's work.

Authentic teacher research such as this requires a shift from our traditional understanding of *teacher*. In my opinion, one of the most significant things we can learn from the educators in Reggio Emilia, Italy, is to shift our understanding and practice from the "knowing it all" teacher to the learning, curious, wonder-filled teacher. This means that we both see ourselves differently and see children differently. Real, lifelong learning will be fresh and new only if we create the conditions as educators for this kind of learning to thrive. This requires an excited teacher who expects to be amazed by how capable, intelligent, and creative children are. We see that this shift has taken place in the minds and hearts of the teacher-authors of this book through their stories of transformation for themselves and their students.

The strength of the community of learners in the study group that authored this book is palpable. We hear about it in every chapter and hear it in every voice. Without this community of supportive learners, the stories you will read here would not be so rich and this book would not be in your hands.

This is another nugget to take from the Reggio approach—this idea of the web of connections between all parts of the system that make up a rich and dynamic learning community. This system encompasses the children and adults, the culture, everyone's ideas, the learning environments, the city, and all the patterns that connect them. In Reggio Emilia, the connections between all these parts form the central, underlying idea of community.

We are and can be inspired by the work of the Reggio Emilia educators, the Italian children, and the community of support in this remarkable northern Italian town. They have always been the first to say they do not recommend that other countries and contexts try to imitate them. Rather, they would like to be one example of what is possible when we truly value children's intelligence and creativity and our future, when we believe that we can create schools as places for meaningful, relevant, lasting learning.

Inventor Charles Kettering wrote:

Research is a high hat word that scares a lot of people. It needn't. It is rather simple. Essentially, research is nothing but a state of mind, a friendly, welcoming attitude toward change. Going out to look for change instead of waiting for it to come. Research is an effort to do things better and not to be caught asleep at the switch. It is the problem-solving mind as contrasted with the leave well enough alone mind. It is the tomorrow mind instead of yesterday mind.

Judith Lysaker and her team of teacher colleagues have given us an inspiring collection of stories that are alive with research and persistence, patience and openness. They have learned about lasting literacy learning, and they have shared what they have learned with grace and skill. May they inspire us all to do the same.

Louise Boyd Cadwell
Author of *Bringing Reggio Emilia Home*

Introduction

Key to all learning is relationships. Learning doesn't happen in a vacuum. A wide range of relationships facilitates inquiry and the teaching–learning processes. These relationships include relationships with people, with materials, with space, with time, and with text. How do these relationships develop? What supports deep relationships from which optimal learning can occur? Putting relationships at the center of my classroom created this opportunity and allowed the time and space for me and the learners to negotiate a curriculum that best met the varied needs of my learners.

—*Karen K. Goldstein*

Becoming a teacher-researcher has changed the way I teach and my thinking about how children learn. The term *research* conjures up thoughts of lab coats, sterile environments, and impartial scientists looking for the facts, the definitive answers in cold hard data. In the classroom just the opposite is true. Research in the classroom is incredibly messy, extremely personal, and the one true answer is never found. I have come to the conclusion that this process of questioning, listening, noticing, and looking back at the learning is essential to my growth as a teacher.

—*Patty Durbin Horan*

I open with these short quotes from contributors Karen K. Goldstein and Patty Durbin Horan because each articulates a central purpose of this book. Karen's words point to what became our group's common topic of inquiry—the role of relationships within Reggio-inspired early childhood literacy environments. Patty reflects on the meaning of teacher research in her life as a classroom teacher, in particular the transformative nature of her experience of engaging in this kind of work. As her words tell us, the process of teacher research led to new personal understandings and a sense of empowerment. These two fundamental ideas—the importance of relationships in children's early literacy learning and the transformative role of teacher inquiry in our lives as teachers—come together in the work we put forward here. Like our colleagues in Reggio Emilia, Italy, we view these two ideas as *integral* to each other; the work and the stance of inquiry are definitional to teaching–learning relationships as they are enacted in daily classroom life (Rinaldi, 2006).

Our teacher research group began informally as a way to support one another as teacher-researchers. We were all conducting classroom-based studies and met as a group to talk about them so that the hard work of data generation and analysis as well as the emotional demands of teacher research could be mediated by the companionship of others. We hoped that if we could meet regularly, this companionship might help us sustain our new, somewhat fragile forays into teacher research.

As we talked on those late, sultry August afternoons, we discovered the joy and comfort of conversation centered on our own evolving questions, our attempts at a rich classroom life, and the children we cared about. We avoided the conversations that tended to absorb us in our buildings: testing, standards, mandates, the latest and greatest strategy or assessment technique. We talked. We talked a lot. We told stories of the children we loved, the children who perplexed us, and the moments that filled us with nearly unmanageable emotion. Those stories were crowded with points of inquiry, where questions would arise like the fog on a pond in the fall, misty not-yet-completely-formed questions full of mystery and the power to provoke our thinking.

Our teacher research group became the place where we engaged these questions. Our shared thinking allowed us to unearth disruptive anomalies, the "puzzling events" (Phillips & Gallas, 2004) of our teaching lives, and allowed us to meet and to know them, rather than allowing them to settle into our bones undiscovered and unexplored. We found we could navigate the fog in the company of others, wonder through the stories, and finally land on our questions long enough to make important discoveries about them. We invited others, and soon we were a developing community of nascent teacher-researchers. Ralph Fletcher tells us that "every teacher must find a place from which to speak" (qtd. in Buckner, 2005, p. xii). Our teacher inquiry group gave us such a place, a place of shared understandings and ongoing caring conversation. This book is the result of finding that place.

As we met and talked, sharing our data and our budding insights, we discovered a developing sense of solidarity and strength. We soon realized that our original purpose for meeting—to support ourselves in the challenges of teacher inquiry—was being superseded by a different set of purposes, purposes more moral and political than practical. We began to consider our work as important not just because we might help one another develop useful insights about young children's literacy learning, but also because we were bringing the voices of children front and center, assigning them new weight, new consequence, and an importance in their own right that was somehow different from anything we had experienced before. We found that we wanted our work to amplify the voices of children so that many more people might hear them and notice their beauty, wisdom, and meaning. We talked about our students as inquirers pursuing their own hypotheses, not only about the worlds they inhabited but also about literacy itself, this new powerful resource for connecting to others and to ideas. We thought of our children as coresearchers as we tried to document and describe our explorations of literacy and curriculum.

We soon came to realize that our work together was a way of providing ourselves with a new kind of professional development, professional development with personal and social authenticity that invited us to adopt new ways of knowing through which to view learning and ourselves as teachers. We weren't simply adding a different set of activities or strategies to our repertoire as teachers; we were experiencing the epistemic shifts of transformative learning (Mezirow & Associates, 2000).

By January our Thursday gatherings had evolved into a coherent group of regulars, all of whom were teachers of young children. Most of us were educated in the Reggio Emilia approach and some had been to Reggio Emilia, Italy, on study trips. All but one of us were from the same school district. This district had recently opened four early learning centers purposefully designed to reflect the principles of education present in the schools of Reggio Emilia. The centers have open spaces, high ceilings, and large windows to bring the natural world inside. In addition, different textures such as block glass walls, large circular concrete tables, textured walls, and glass classroom dividers support thinking and provoke curiosity. Curricula rich in project-based learning experiences, literacy workshops, and opportunities for artistic expression were encouraged by building principals and provided for with large blocks of uninterrupted time. We shared a commitment to the idea that children are capable, competent, active learners who have their own inquiries and are filled with ongoing and developing hypotheses about the world; a conceptualization of environment as teacher; an inquiry perspective on curriculum; and a view of relationships as important to learning. These principles directly influenced our early childhood classrooms and are discussed in more detail in Chapter 1.

We also shared a commitment to our understanding of teachers and teaching in Reggio, where research and teaching go hand in hand and where teachers are viewed as intellectually competent and politically empowered. For us this meant that being Reggio inspired wasn't just about children, but about us and our view of ourselves as teachers. We were challenged to more seriously consider the idea that our children's talk, actions, ideas, and play are worthy of our research, and that our careful attention and documentation of children's learning is all part of good teaching. We were challenged to take ourselves seriously and embrace the belief that our time is worthy of the pursuit of our own questions, the demands of data generation and analysis, and the development of new understandings.

At the same time, our district involved us in reform efforts aimed at bringing writers workshop (Calkins, 1994; Ray & Cleveland, 2004) into our districts. We became interested in readers workshop also, inspired by our own work with writers workshop and school visits by Lester Laminack. We devoured books and articles by literacy experts such as Lucy Calkins (1994), Katie Wood Ray (Ray & Cleveland, 2004), Kathy Collins (2004), and Cathy Mere (2005), as well as by researchers like Elizabeth Sulzby (1991). "Little books" for writing were filling our classrooms, kindergartners were inventing their own version of readers workshop, and projects were flourishing.

What were the connections between the curricular construct of workshop and our Reggio-inspired beliefs? How could we make sense of the commonalities and points of difference to deepen our pedagogy? How would articulating the life of "workshop" in a Reggio-inspired environment bring new life to our understandings of young children as learners, inquirers, and literate people? These are the questions we have pursued and which we explore in the following chapters.

The purpose of this book is to share our investigations of enacting literacy workshops in Reggio-inspired environments. These investigations consist of both content—the ideas that we developed, particularly around relationships— and process—the ways in which we developed these ideas through the practice of teacher research. To reflect these two prongs, this book is organized by chapters in which each teacher research project is described by the teacher-author, followed by a section called "Research Conversations." In these accompanying sections, I talk with each of the teachers about her work, focusing on a particular aspect of the inquiry process that was most central to her research. We include these conversations because they illustrate the ways in which teacher research became personally relevant classroom practice that connected us to children and to our own growing knowledge. It is our hope that these dialogues make the processes—the relational action of teacher research—more visible and therefore more useful to others.

In Chapter 1, "First There Was Reggio," I provide a more detailed background on the philosophy that supports teachers' work in Reggio Emilia, Italy.

Specifically, I describe the belief system and practices that inspired us as teachers in the US Midwest. In addition, I summarize our view of workshop and the people who have made a difference in our thinking about literacy.

In Chapter 2, Amanda Angle begins the presentation of teacher research studies. As a kindergarten teacher concerned with the reduction of time available for play in the kindergarten schedule, Amanda sets out to observe, document, and describe the ways in which children use play as a tool across the curricular structures of project work and workshop to develop literate capacity and skill. In her study, "Project Work Meets Workshop through Play in a Kindergarten Classroom," Amanda uses developmental play theory to understand the importance of play and imagination to provoke the uses and practices of literacy within project work. She asks the question, "In what ways do kindergarten children use play to develop understandings and become literate beings?"

In Chapter 3, Karen K. Goldstein tells the story of a five-year-old English language learner who navigated his way to literacy in a monolingual kindergarten setting using blocks as a context for meaning making. While narrating his journey of becoming part of this English-speaking community, she also tells us of Eric's influence on her own journey, in which she becomes a teacher-researcher and political advocate for all children. Karen documents and describes these parallel journeys in her study of language learning, "Building Identity as a Language Learner: How Reggio Foundations Inspired Workshop Flexibility."

In Chapter 4, Patty Durbin Horan describes her use of teacher research and the practice of reading aloud to build a peaceful community during a difficult year. Inspired by the work of our Italian colleagues, Patty set out to view her classroom as, first and foremost, "a place of relationships," and to investigate the ways in which reading aloud might strengthen and bring children together. "Navigating Rough Waters with Read-Alouds" tells a story of transformation for both teacher and children as they used stories to develop more peaceful relationships with one another.

In Chapter 5, "Thinking across the Curriculum: The Importance of Children's Connections to Peers, Materials, and Home," Alyssa Hildebrand examines the ways in which children's thinking becomes visible in her Reggio-inspired workshop settings. Informed by the Italian educators' focus on relationships, the negotiation of curriculum, a supportive social atmosphere, and a pedagogy of the environment, she describes three kinds of relationships that her kindergarten children draw on as "thinking tools" as they develop as thinkers and authors in writers workshop.

In Chapter 6, Jennifer Wheat studies the ways in which relationships support literacy learning in her multiage K–1 classroom. In "The Power of Relationships," she explores this idea through observation and "layers of writing," focusing on one child as a case study to describe the complex web of relation-ships that supported him in his literacy learning. Framing her thinking about relationships with ideas from both Reggio Emilia educators and Donna Skol-nick, Jennifer asserts that Thomas's relationships with the classroom environ-ment and materials were his entry point into the curriculum, and that peer relationships provided the critical scaffolding that sustained these relationships.

Kristin Scibienski looks closely at the development of readers in her readers workshop in Chapter 7, "A Look at Cultural Tools in a Reggio-Inspired Kinder-garten Readers Workshop," investigating the particular aspects of environment that appear to support emergent readers' use of this curricular structure. Focus-ing on the Reggio principles of "environment as third teacher," "relationships as mediation," and "cultural tools," Kristin analyzes her students' reading work, asking, "In what ways do children use cultural tools during readers workshop and how does their use relate to literacy development?"

In Chapter 8, "Our Pedagogical Experiment," I sum up our developing views of "relationship" within Reggio-inspired workshop environments and articulate an integrated view of relational pedagogy that grew out of our collective inves-tigations. We call this integrated view *relationality* and define it as "the living out of a complex set of intersubjective relationships within the classroom commu-nity." Grounded in this view, I argue for a revaluing of the human dimensions of early learning to push back against the pervasive culture of achievement that currently holds sway in early childhood classrooms.

Bibliography

Bruner, J. (1986). *Actual minds, possible worlds*. Cambridge, MA: Harvard University Press.

Buckner, A. (2005). *Notebook know-how: Strategies for the writer's notebook*. Portland, ME: Stenhouse.

Calkins, L. M. (1994). *The art of teaching writing* (new ed.). Portsmouth, NH: Heinemann.

Collins, K. (2004). *Growing readers: Units of study in the primary classroom*. Portland, ME: Stenhouse.

Dyson, A. (1993). *Social worlds of children learning to read and write in an urban primary school*. New York: Teachers College Press.

Gallas, K. (1994). *The languages of learning: How children talk, write, dance, draw, and sing their understanding of the world.* New York: Teachers College Press.

Mere, C. (2005). *More than guided reading: Finding the right instructional mix, K–3.* Portland, ME: Stenhouse.

Mezirow, J., & Associates. (2000). *Learning as transformation: Critical perspectives on a theory in progress.* San Francisco: Jossey-Bass.

Palmer, P. J. (1998). *The courage to teach: Exploring the inner landscape of a teacher's life.* San Francisco: Jossey-Bass.

Phillips, A., & Gallas, K. (2004). Introduction. Developing a community of inquiry: The values and practices of the Brookline Teacher Researcher Seminar (pp. 1–11). In C. Ballenger (Ed.), *Regarding children's words: Teacher research on language and literacy.* New York: Teachers College Press.

Ray, K. W., & Cleveland, L. B. (2004). *About the authors: Writing workshop with our youngest writers.* Portsmouth, NH: Heinemann.

Rinaldi, C. (2006). *In dialogue with Reggio Emilia: Listening, researching and learning.* New York: Routledge.

Sulzby, E. (1991). Assessment of emergent literacy: Storybook reading. *The Reading Teacher, 44*(7), 498–500.

Vygotsky, L. S. (1986). *Thought and language.* Cambridge, MA, MIT Press.

Wertsch, J. V. (1984). The zone of proximal development: Some conceptual issues. *New Directions for Child and Adolescent Development, 1984*(23), 7–18.

First There Was Reggio

Judith T. Lysaker

The pedagogic experience of Reggio Emilia is a story so far spanning more than 40 years that can be described as a pedagogical experiment in a whole community.

—Dalhberg & Moss (2006, p. 3)

Historical and Political Contexts of the Reggio Approach

The Reggio approach to early childhood education grew out of a response to the devastation of the Second World War in Italy. Parents, primarily mothers, in the town of Reggio Emilia, located in northern Italy, were determined that nothing like that war would ever happen again. They believed that the place to begin building a new peaceful world, one in which fascism could not gain a foothold, was with the education of children. So the community of Reggio built municipal schools dedicated to the education of children that were energized by a new liberalism, progressive educational thought, and a burgeoning women's movement. In this way, the Reggio approach—its founding beliefs and purposes—is intimately tied to the place that is Reggio Emilia, Italy. Reggio parents and educators established a caring community in which the dignity of all children and their engagement in that community and in the world were encouraged and honored.

Basic Tenets of the Reggio Approach

Grounded in political and social ideologies, the new municipal schools of Reggio quickly embarked on a particular set of pedagogies that grew out of them, and the "pedagogical experiment" was begun. Under the leadership of Loris Malaguzzi, the educators of Reggio explored a set of educational practices grounded in an interdisciplinary framework that drew on social constructivist learning theories, principles of architectural design, and philosophical assumptions about beauty and love. Reggio educators were influenced by the thinking of Dewey, Piaget, Vygotsky, and others who emphasized the child as an active learner, one who thrives on engagement with others and with the environment. Likewise, the teacher was also seen as engaged with others and the classroom environment, particularly through research (Cadwell, 2003). Later, Jerome Bruner and Howard Gardner were visitors and influences on the development of the Reggio approach. Gardner sums up the Reggio approach in his introduction to *The Hundred Languages of Children*:

> The Reggio system can be described succinctly as follows: It is a collection of schools for young children in which each child's intellectual, emotional, social and moral potentials are carefully cultivated and guided. The principal educational vehicle involves youngsters in long-term engrossing projects, which are carried out in a beautiful, healthy, love-filled setting. (qtd. in Edwards, Gandini, & Forman, 1998, p. xvi)

The Reggio approach is thus both a philosophic and a pedagogic approach to the education of young children that rests on the central ideas, summarized here from Cadwell (2003): (1) an image of the child as protagonist, collaborator, communicator, coteacher, and coresearcher; (2) the environment as "third educator" in the classroom along with the teacher and the child, one that sets up conditions for learning; (3) the teacher as partner, nurturer, guide, and researcher; (4) the valuing of multiple languages that children use to make sense of their world; and (5) an inquiry approach to curriculum in which meaningful, relevant learning unfolds with accompanying documentation supporting and communicating that learning.

From these elements organically at play in the classroom rises what is called the "pedagogy of listening." This is, as Rinaldi (2006) describes it, "an ethical relationship of openness to the 'other,' trying to listen to the 'other' from his or her own position and experience and not treating the other as the same" (p. 15). For us this means that relationships become the sine qua non, the nonnegotiable, the critical pivot of everything that happens and might happen in our classrooms. We believe that as teachers, when we are able to listen, to take an empathetic stance, good teaching happens. We work as Noddings (2005) tells us, to "apprehend the reality of the other" (p. 14) with the expectation that the other will not be like us.

Image of the Child

As we learned about the ideas and practices developed in Reggio schools, certain aspects of the Reggio approach became important to our thinking. First we found ourselves influenced greatly by what is referred to as "the image of the child," addressed by Carlina Rinaldi:

> One of the focal points of the Reggio Emilia philosophy, as Loris Malaguzzi wrote, is the image of a child who, right from the moment of birth is so engaged in developing a relationship with the world and intent on experiencing the world that he develops a complex system of abilities, learning strategies and ways of organizing relationships. He produces change and dynamic movement in the systems in which he is involved, including the family, the society and the school. A product of culture, values and rights, competent in living and learning (2006, p. 83).

Like our Italian colleagues, our image of the child is one in which children are resourceful, competent constructors of knowledge and active agents in pursuit of their own understandings. We assume that as active agents, children have their own inquiries, that they develop ongoing hypotheses about the world, and that they are the best informants for our teaching. In our classrooms and our research, we saw them as coteachers, coresearchers, and curriculum collaborators as we jointly investigated questions and constructed the structures for learning in our classrooms.

This image of the child naturally led us to think about children's rights—the right to learn in ways that make sense to them; the right to exist in a system of nurturing relationships. This view of children was particularly important to us as teachers who wanted to push back against the No Child Left Behind Act, with its focus on teacher-directed classrooms and deficit views of young children.

Teacher as Researcher

In a related vein, we embraced a strong image of the teacher. In the Reggio approach, the teacher is viewed as an active agent in pursuit of personal understandings about teaching and learning and is considered a competent professional capable of producing knowledge through research. At the outset of our work together, we were most familiar with one aspect of research, the practice of documentation. The Reggio Emilia approach views documentation as the ongoing and indispensable work of making children's learning visible and public. Documentation involves the careful collection of children's work, the meticulous recording of their thinking, and the construction of a visual record of the work of the class. Each of us had constructed documentation panels—large boards on which we arranged children's data, in a way that both made their learning visible and appealing and placed their voices vibrantly and prominently in our classrooms and in the hallways of our buildings.

However, perhaps most critical to us as a teacher research group and what pushed us to take our own thinking more seriously was the Reggio recognition that teachers are *theorists*.

> Reggio's theories are rich and provocative, not least the pedagogy of listening and the hundred languages. But at the same time, Reggio challenges the "arrogant idea of the continuing separation between theory and practice," arguing that they are inseparable—one without the other is inconceivable. By so doing, Reggio also revalues the practitioner, indeed questions the very term as implying that there can and should be a distinction between those who practice and those who theorize. (Rinaldi, 2006, p. 17)

We began to view our role as thinkers and researchers as integral to who we were as teachers, and to more earnestly consider our abilities to generate ideas from our classroom work.

We were also beginning to navigate the teacher research literature and found colleagues in people such as Ruth Hubbard and Brenda Power (2003), Karen Gallas (1994, 2003), and Karen Hankins (2003), who document and describe the work of teacher-researchers. From Hubbard and Power (2003) we learned that our worries about teaching, the things that caused us to question what we were doing, or why, were worthy of exploration and of systematic study. Karen Gallas (1994, 2003) taught us that our research journals constituted data, that deep thinking could come from them, and that like the documentation of children's work, our research journals could make teaching and learning visible. Karen Hankins (2003) helped us to see there was an important place for the personal as well as the theoretical in our research, and added to the Reggio definition of *teacher as researcher* by bringing the personhood of the teacher into research alongside the personhood of the child. All of this fit with our new dedication to teacher research and our developing identities as intellectually competent and politically empowered coresearchers.

Environment as Teacher

In addition to these new conceptions of ourselves and our students, we found the idea of "environment as third educator" compelling and useful. This notion suggests that children learn not only from each other and their teacher but also from the objects, materials, and features of the spaces that surround them. Materials and objects have particular affordances; they make certain kinds of learning possible. We valued the idea that the classroom environment within which young children work and play should feel safe and comfortable, have beauty and inspire learning, and be a place to grow into themselves as complex human beings. So we redesigned our classrooms as aesthetic spaces, environments of beauty as well as utility, dynamic spaces that invite interaction and relation. Inspired by our Italian colleagues, we built collections of natural materials and interesting objects for children to explore, draw, and manipulate. We placed mirrors and light tables in our classrooms, which allowed children to play with the physics of light, space, and shadow.

Our interest in early literacy also led us to Brian Cambourne (1995) and his conditions for natural language learning. We considered the notions of immersion, demonstration, and engagement and found them compatible with our Reggio-inspired views. Our classroom environments would immerse children in literacy practices, provide ongoing demonstrations of language use, and offer opportunities for relevant literacy engagements. Cambourne's concept of approximation was particularly helpful as we prepared environments that would support risk taking, environments in which children could construct their own versions of reading and writing as legitimate in their own right. We filled our classrooms with tubs of books for children to explore, to get to know, and to use as "teachers of reading." We created inviting spaces for young writers, complete with a broad array of writing materials and utensils. We also made sure that these environments contained spaces for dialogue between ourselves and the children as well as between and among children.

Inquiry Approach to Curriculum

Our teacher research group adopted the idea that curriculum unfolds because it is driven by inquiry. Often this inquiry is represented by sustained, child-centered projects in which children and teachers collaboratively pursue a topic of genuine interest that arises out of the daily experiences of children. As Gandini (1997) states,

> Projects provide the backbone of the children's and teacher's learning experiences. They are based on the strong conviction that learning by doing is of great importance and that to discuss in groups and to revisit ideas and experiences is the premier way of gaining better understanding and learning. (p. 22)

The driving force behind children's curiosities and inquiries in the curriculum was familiar to us from Dewey (1938), who advocates for the child as an active constructor of his or her own knowledge through experience. We had read Katz and Chard's (2000) work on the project approach and had experienced the curricular power of children's projects in our own classrooms. Our literacy education background included Short and Harste's (1996) *Creating Classrooms for Authors and Inquirers* in which the notion of inquiry is applied and integrated with the work of learning to read and write. Our conversations included thinking about literacy as a project itself, an intense, self-motivated investigation of learning to read and write.

Relationships

Finally, our Reggio influences led us to allow ourselves to revalue relationships as underlying all learning. Like many teachers of young children, we were already won over by the importance of our relationships with children, parents, and families and of children's relationships with one another. The sociocultural views of Vygotsky (1978) influenced our thinking about the essential relational quality of all learning, particularly literacy learning. The idea of scaffolding suggests that all learning happens when a more able other mediates the learning through language and through the use of materials. This common idea gained even more credence as we viewed it from our Reggio lens. In addition, many of us were familiar with Donna Skolnick's (2000) work, which outlines a set of relationships that teachers might consider when planning for literacy learning: teacher to curriculum, child to curriculum, teacher to child, and child to child. All of this led us to consider relationships as the first and foremost concern of teaching, and so the promotion and facilitation of children's relationships with us, with one another, and with materials in the environment became critical.

And Then There Was Workshop

Working within this set of beliefs, we were introduced to the workshop approach to literacy (Calkins, 1994; Ray & Cleveland, 2004). After learning the structures and tone of workshop teaching, we set up our classrooms so that the supports for workshop were ever present, through the availability of beautiful and just-right books, a variety of small teacher-constructed blank books, and a wealth of material for drawing and writing. We began our workshop teaching with the simple and predictable structures suggested by Calkins:

Mini-Lessons. We began each readers and writers workshop with a mini-lesson that provided a focused look at some aspect of reading or writing. We decided on the topics for mini-lessons based on our observations of our students, as well as from our reading of authors like Katie Wood Ray and Lisa Cleveland (2004). Most often our lessons addressed a teaching point through the purposeful use of children's literature. Inspired by Ray and others, we referred to these as mentor texts. We regularly photocopied the covers of mentor texts, labeled them for what they offered us as writers, and displayed them at the children's eye level. The material of text became a valued and lovely way of supporting skill and strategy development in our young students. Often our mini-lessons were organized into units of study that allowed us to stay with a particular idea or author for an extended period.

Independent Reading/Writing. Mini-lessons were followed by independent reading or independent writing, though we found that our students often effectively merged the two. In our early childhood classrooms, independent workshop time was neither silent nor independent. Children worked as readers and writers by reading and thinking aloud, by helping one another, and often by inventing new and interesting ways of co-reading and co-writing. During this time, we held reading and writing conferences and documented these conferences through anecdotal notes and other teacher-created record-keeping strategies.

Share Time. Independent reading and writing ended with share time. Children often gathered together at a carpeted area in front of a big book easel and whiteboard to talk about their reading and writing work of the day. If writing had been the focus, we used share time to have the children read their work to peers and get feedback from their young collaborators. As teachers we used this time instructionally. We noticed aloud, in front of and with the children, what the author had done well that day as a writer. Similarly, at the end of a workshop focused on reading, children volunteered to tell their peers about what they had accomplished as readers that day. And with careful teacher responses, we acknowledged and built up the good reading work the students had done.

Our Own Pedagogic Experiment

Within this pedagogic richness, questions about literacy and, in particular, the use of readers and writers workshops within our Reggio-inspired environments arose loudly. After all, the Reggio approach is in large part an approach to very young children, who are not necessarily at the point of being print focused. In fact, we noticed very little specific attention to reading and writing in the Reggio classrooms we visited in Italy. How would this set of beliefs fit with our American dedication to promoting the development of readers and writers in kindergarten classrooms? What were the connections between these approaches to curriculum?

As we considered these questions, how we might pursue them and to what end, our distant colleagues in Italy once again came to mind. In Reggio Emilia, educators refer to their innovative practices as their "pedagogical experiment" (Dahlberg & Moss, 2006, p. 3). We were inspired by the qualities of this work: (1) the unequivocal focus on understanding children's thinking and children's being as the primary source of curricular design and (2) the active intellectual role of teachers in making pedagogic decisions based on observations of children. As we met in our study group, we began to see that our inquiry into readers and writers workshops within Reggio-inspired early childhood environments was becoming our own pedagogical experiment.

Our shared backgrounds, eagerness to learn from children, and questioning spirits drew us closer together. Each week we lugged our bags brimming with "raw data" to study group meetings. We thrived on the conversations about data, the children, our questions, and how to pursue those questions. We began to play with data-generation, collection, and management strategies and supported one another in our modest initial attempts. As we learned about our students and about ourselves as researchers, we found that we returned to our classrooms more hopeful and more dedicated to the work of inquiry with children.

Over the course of two years, we engaged in our pedagogical experiment, studying the curricular structures of readers and writers workshop, as well as the idea and structure of project work, and immersed ourselves in the social constructivist views of early literacy that are foundational to these curricular structures. We worked with Vygotsky's (1978) ideas of mediation and the zone of proximal development. We considered the meanings of "relational potentials" and "quality of space" suggested by Carlina Rinaldi (2006), and wondered how we could break open those ideas with Parker Palmer's (1983, 1998) work on relationship and community. We began to notice that the Reggio principles we embraced highlighted and accentuated particular aspects of readers and writers workshop for us, adding new dimensions to the ways in which we regarded the meaning making and authoring of our students. Our image of the child as capable and competent, our regard for the role of the environment in learning, and the importance of relationships took on new meanings as we experimented with readers and writers workshop.

We started to view the documentation of children's learning as a vital part of the literacy environment, a personally relevant provocation for literacy learning and for the development of authoring in our emergent readers and writers. We began to understand inquiry both as a central characteristic of the active learner and as a way of *relating* to others and to the world. We saw children's inquiry into the world of text in particular as the driving force of literacy learning in our workshop classrooms. Most important, we began to notice the web of relationships that constituted our classroom communities in ways we had not before. Children's relationships with people (both peers and adults), materials (particularly texts), the environment (particularly documentation), as well as children's developing relation to the processes, practices, and "idea" of literacy, took on new and substantive meanings as we immersed ourselves in this pedagogical experiment of working with readers and writers workshop in our already established Reggio-inspired classrooms.

As we talked about these ideas, something of our own, something we have come to call "relationality," began to take shape. We were aware that the relational perspective we were developing was a kind of synthesis of our particular encounters with social constructivism. At the core of our beliefs, however, was the idea that *relationships* broadly defined were the most compelling, complex, and important aspect of the classrooms we had and the classrooms we wanted to have—not *relationships* defined in some clinical, neutral way; rather, relationships driven by love, care, and making sense of the world with and for others. Thus, we found ourselves launched into a kind of meta-study of the relational as we each pursued our own teacher research project. As a group, our work converges on this particular set of ideas, with each piece of teacher research highlighting some aspect of our developing relational perspective.

Bibliography

Cadwell, L. B. (2003). *Bringing learning to life: The Reggio approach to early childhood education.* New York: Teachers College Press.

Calkins, L. M. (1994). *The art of teaching writing* (new ed.). Portsmouth, NH: Heinemann.

Cambourne, B. (1995). Towards an educationally relevant theory of language learning: Twenty years of inquiry. *The Reading Teacher, 49*(3), 182–190.

Dahlberg, G., & Moss, P. (2006). Introduction: Our Reggio Emilia. In, C. Rinaldi, *In dialogue with Reggio Emilia: Listening, researching and learning* (pp. 1–22). New York: Routledge.

Dewey, J. (1938). *Experience and education.* New York: Macmillan.

Edwards, C., Gandini, L., & Forman, G. (Eds.). (1998). *The hundred languages of children: The Reggio Emilia approach—advanced reflections* (2nd ed.). Greenwich, CT: Ablex.

Gallas, K. (1994). *The languages of learning: How children talk, write, dance, draw, and sing their understanding of the world.* New York: Teachers College Press.

Gallas, K. (2003). *Imagination and literacy: A teacher's search for the heart of learning.* New York: Teachers College Press.

Gandini, L. (1997). Foundations of the Reggio Emilia approach. In J. Hendrick (Ed.), *First steps toward teaching the Reggio way* (pp.14–25). Upper Saddle River, NJ: Prentice Hall.

Hankins, K. H. (2003). *Teaching through the storm: A journal of hope.* New York: Teachers College Press.

Hubbard, R. S., & Power, B. M. (2003). *The art of classroom inquiry: A handbook for teacher-researchers* (rev. ed.). Portsmouth, NH: Heinemann.

Katz, L. G., & Chard, S. C. (2000). *Engaging children's minds: The project approach* (2nd ed.). Stanford, CT: Ablex.

Noddings, N. (2005). *The challenge to care in schools: An alternative approach to education* (2nd ed.). New York: Teachers College Press.

Palmer, P. J. (1983). *To know as we are known: A spirituality of education.* San Francisco: Harper and Row.

Palmer, P. J. (1998). *The courage to teach: Exploring the inner landscape of a teacher's life.* San Francisco: Jossey-Bass.

Ray, K. W., & Cleveland, L. B. (2004). *About the authors: Writing workshop with our youngest writers.* Portsmouth, NH: Heinemann.

Rinaldi, C. (2006). *In dialogue with Reggio Emilia: Listening, researching and learning.* New York: Routledge.

Short, K. G., & Harste, J. C. (with Burke, C.). (1996). *Creating classrooms for authors and inquirers* (2nd ed.). Portsmouth, NH: Heinemann.

Skolnick, D. (2000). *More than meets the eye: How relationships enhance literacy learning.* Portsmouth, NH: Heinemann.

Vygotsky, L. S. (1978). *Mind in society: The development of higher psychological processes.* Cambridge, MA: Harvard University Press.

Vygotsky, L. S. (1986). *Thought and language.* Cambridge, MA, MIT Press.

Project Work Meets Workshop through Play in a Kindergarten Classroom

AMANDA ANGLE

*P*lay is a common word and one that is very familiar to most early childhood educators. Unfortunately, despite its familiarity, academic demands of the "new kindergarten" (Hatch, 2005) make play more and more difficult to include in the kindergarten curriculum (Da Ros-Voseles, Danyi, & Aurillo, 2003). Because of the constant pressure to raise standardized test scores, playtime is being pushed out of daily classroom life for kindergarten children.

As a kindergarten teacher, I have had many opportunities to see children play and have come to value the importance of play for children's development. In light of the need to defend play, I began to wonder what role play might have in children's learning, particularly in children's inquiries and their literacy development. This chapter reflects the teaching and research done in my kindergarten classroom over one year. The question that guided this work was: *In what ways do kindergarten children use their play to pursue inquiry, develop understandings, and become literate beings?*

Context

Like others in my study group, I teach in a public kindergarten that is housed in an early learning center within a metropolitan area. Like my colleagues, I embrace much of the philosophy behind the Reggio schools discussed in Chapter 1.

The pedagogical principle that was most important to me as a teacher at the time of this study was the image of the child. When I view children as competent, curious protagonists in their own learning, it makes sense for them to be important collaborators with me in constructing curriculum. Another significant belief for my work culled from the Reggio approach is the importance of the environment as a teacher. To me this means that the environment "makes room" for children to be active in their own learning. The physical environment of my classroom is child centered, with many open spaces set aside for building, playing, and exploring materials. In addition to these physical characteristics, aspects of environment such as talk and activity are critical supports that shape learning. I am particularly interested in play as an environmental influence on learning.

Finally, inquiry-oriented projects, in which children pursue interests over time, are part of my Reggio-inspired environment. The belief that supports this approach to curriculum—that children learn by doing—is one we embrace in my district. In addition to our Reggio background, we have also studied Sylvia Chard's (1994) project approach to extend our knowledge of an inquiry curriculum. In my classroom, I look for and respond to children's interests in ways that I hope will help them pursue topics and ideas they are curious about. Like the others in our study group, I use the curricular structures of readers and writers workshops, which I believe also reflect a strong image of the child as well as the idea that children learn by doing.

Data Collection

In terms of demographics, the children in this study represent diverse races and ethnic groups as well as all levels of the socioeconomic spectrum. Almost one-fourth of my students spoke Spanish as their first language.

I collected various forms of data for my study. First, I took photographs throughout my study to highlight different examples of how the children were using play to support their inquiries and literacy development. Second, I collected student artifacts that showed the literacy learning happening during our projects. Some examples of student artifacts include books the children created that related to our projects and written labels made for block sculptures. I also took anecdotal notes on a daily basis. Many of these notes consisted of direct quotations of children's language (see the "Research Conversations" at the end of the chapter). I also took anecdotal notes of the children's actions.

When it was time to analyze my data, I first organized it by separating our bug project data from our airplane project data. I then read and reread my data to identify patterns and connections across the two projects, looking specifically for patterns connected to play that I could use to show others how children were using play to support learning. When it came time to start writing, I decided to use a narrative approach; I wanted readers to be able to picture the play in my classroom. In fact, narrative is a common way for teachers to share their teacher research (Hankins, 2003). Here is the first of my two stories.

Project Meets Workshop through Play: Bugs

CHILD 1: Look, Miss Angle! There is a bug on the floor by your desk!

CHILD 2: What is it?

CHILD 3: I think it is a beetle!

CHILD 1: Hurry, can we catch it? We can have another class pet!

CHILD 2: What should we name it?

This conversation took place one day in early September as the school year was beginning. Our class had just come in from the playground when a small group of students noticed something very small and black crawling on the floor by my desk. As much as I disliked bugs and insects, the children's excitement made their interest impossible to ignore. After finding the small beetle, which was quickly named Carl, the children were on a mission to find as many bugs as possible for our room! Little did I know that we were beginning an intense investigation of bugs that would turn into a semester-long literacy-rich project, one that would spill into our readers and writers workshops. The playful act of finding "Carl" proved to be the provocation that launched some critical literacy learning for my students.

I began gathering as many books as I could find on insects. Soon we had tubs and tubs of books about different bugs. Children's questions filled the room. "What is an insect? What do beetles eat? Where do insects live? How many kinds of insects are there?" I posted the children's questions on large chart paper in a prominent place in the room where we could refer to them repeatedly.

Bugs and Books

The children began bug research naturally and intensely. During readers workshop, we were reading books such as *Bugs, Bugs, Bugs!* by Bob Barner, *I Love Spiders* by John Parker, *Bugs* by Nancy Winslow Parker and Joan Richards Wright, *The Best Book of Bugs* by Claire Llewellyn, and *About Insects* by Cathryn Sill. During independent reading, children read alone and with one another to find answers to the questions we had posted earlier on our chart.

Before this, I had begun the practice of using "little books," teacher- or child-made blank paper booklets, to encourage young writers. Now the children began making little books about bugs during workshop. The project work guided mini-lessons on generating questions, finding facts, and comparing and contrasting insects. Of course, many of the children's books were nonfiction and filled with their newfound knowledge. But some children were writing fictional stories and using the different kinds of bugs they were learning about as characters. Project work had completely merged with workshop.

Along with creating books and the playful fantasy about Carl, the children kept working to find more bugs outside around the school. Their list of questions kept growing. At one time we had between ten and fifteen different kinds of bugs in our room: spiders, crickets, grasshoppers, beetles, and a praying mantis affectionately called Sunshine. In fact, every bug we caught received a name that same day, determined by a class vote.

These new, tiny members of our class received lots of attention. The children were constantly drawing pictures and writing notes for the bugs, and stacks of these communications soon piled up, which posed an organizational problem. But, believing that problems can become new provocations for learning, I asked the children, "What can we do with all of these notes?" Immediately they suggested that we make each bug its own mailbox for all of their "mail." Mailbox construction became another daily event that provided important literacy experiences. Once a week we took all the notes out of the mailboxes and read them to the bugs.

CHILD 1: We are making so much stuff for Carl and Sunshine! We need to make them mailboxes to put it all in!

CHILD 2: I am sorting the mail for Carl and Sunshine!

The pictures and notes the children made for the bugs during their play in project work and workshop provided important practice for my emergent readers and writers. The children were constantly using oral and written language together when creating mail for the bugs. Even children who were not yet able to write all the words to represent their thoughts were able to express them through talk and pictures. My view of children as capable and competent, as well as the ongoing data collection of my teacher research, helped me to see and value the important learning that was happening in these children's playful approach to project work and workshop.

Bugs and Blocks

CHILD 1: We need to build a bigger bug house for Carl!

CHILD 2: Can we paint some blocks for our new bug house? We need to paint the blocks for the bug house! It has to be perfect for Carl!

Children continued their play by launching Bug City in the block area for the bugs. They decided we needed to write a letter to our assistant principal to see if it was okay to paint some blocks. With her permission, we immediately got busy.

CHILD 1: We need to lay the blocks down in the front!

CHILD 2: If we don't we won't be able to see Carl!

CHILD 3: Come on! We need to work together!

CHILD 4: I knew if we painted the blocks the bug house would be perfect!

Building Bug City provided ample opportunities for the children to have meaningful play experiences to support their literacy development. During this play, a great deal of interesting talk took place. Children were learning about bugs and using content-rich vocabulary to make sense of what a bug city might look like. This purposeful use of oral language in the building of Bug City is perhaps the most obvious example of children practicing literacy in their play. But the representation of Bug City shows something even greater. In building Bug City from blocks, the children used a variety of materials, including blocks and math manipulatives, to create a visual representation of what they envisioned as a Bug City. They then used this representation to talk about their creation. The blocks and math materials represented a city—one thing stood for another—just as letters, words, and sentences work together to represent meaning in a book. These symbolic play experiences were helping children understand the central concept of written language.

Bug Restaurant

Bug City became a provocation for the next major step of our bug project—the creation of the Bug Food Restaurant. After constructing many different Bug Cities with various restaurants, the children decided that we needed to turn our entire dramatic play center into our very own Bug Food Restaurant.

CHILD 1: We could make the restaurant like this. I want there to be a water fountain!

CHILD 2: We have to make a refrigerator! It is for the food!

CHILD 3: I want the restaurant to look like this!

CHILD 4: What if the bug wants a drink? Maybe he can use this cup for the drink! I am so smart!

CHILD 5: I think the bugs will want chicken too.

CHILD 2: We need some owners to wash the tables.

CHILD 1: We need wallpaper and a nice floor for the restaurant.

CHILD 4: This can be the grasshopper town!

CHILD 3: This can be where all of the neighbors live.

CHILD 1: We need to have a menu.

CHILD 4: What is the name going to be for our restaurant?

CHILD 3: I am trying to think of an idea. Hmmm . . . maybe "Bug Food"?

The creation of the Bug Food Restaurant, just like Bug City, provided a playful context that supported children in becoming accomplished literate beings. They had many opportunities to exchange and compare their own experiences of restaurants through talk. In addition, they did a great deal of reading and writing during play-infused project work and workshop. For example, the children made "Open" and "Closed" signs because the restaurant could not be open all day long!

A particularly rich literacy experience presented itself when the children decided that the Bug Food Restaurant needed a menu. After making a list of food and drinks they wanted the restaurant to serve, the children had to figure out how to sort the items so the menu would make sense. We then searched online together to find pictures to match all of our menu items. Finally, the children decided that we also needed to make multiple copies of the menu because no restaurant has only one.

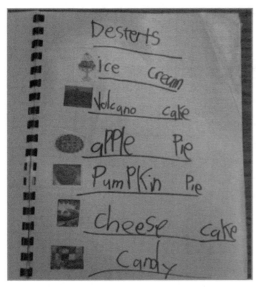

Bug Food Menu

But the influence of the Bug House Restaurant on literacy work didn't end there. The students decided that they wanted to use the menu items to create an ABC chart: *A* stood for apple pie, *B* stood for bread, and so on. This alphabet chart gained relevance and practical value because it was now grounded in the bug project and because the children themselves had created it. We hung it in our room, where it was used daily as a resource for reading and writing.

Throughout the course of the project, the class spent many hours "playing restaurant." Because the children had created so many texts, this play involved regular reading and writing. Naturally, over time the excitement died down.

However, even after many conversations as a class, the children did not want to turn the Bug Food Restaurant into anything else. Even when their interests had moved elsewhere and only a few children played in this area every day, they were not ready to say goodbye to their creation. This shows the power of play to allow children to create their own personally relevant curriculum. They provided their own scaffolds. They reconstructed the organization of the school day by merging their inquiry about bugs and restaurants with readers and writers workshops. This changed the way we used time, so that reading and writing were happening across the day and not just in workshop.

Alphabet Chart

Numerous meaningful literacy learning opportunities became available to the children with these changes.

Project Time Meets Workshop, Round Two: Airplanes

CHILD 1: How do you make a paper airplane?

CHILD 2: I can't figure out how to fold it.

CHILD 3: Look! Mine won't even fly!

CHILD 4: What is a paper airplane suppose to look like?

CHILD 1: How do you make it fly?

CHILD 2: Can someone help me?

Before I knew it, the entire class was surrounding a small round table, everyone working frantically on the puzzle of how to make a paper airplane. I was not sure who started this conversation or where it was headed. But with so many children interested in this quest to make a paper airplane, and with the energy of their conversation, I had the feeling that something useful might develop. So of course I grabbed my notebook and camera and sat in the back to listen and watch closely and to look for opportunities to facilitate learning.

I observed the students for almost two weeks to see if their interest in airplanes was worth pursuing through a more deliberate inquiry, in which I would take a more active role. Then, one Monday morning during our group time on the carpet, I talked to the children directly about what I had seen. I told them about the things I had noticed during their airplane play and showed them the many photographs I had taken of their paper airplane construction. Before I could say much, hands were flying in the air. It seemed as though everyone had something to say. I quickly grabbed chart paper and began recording their comments and questions. By the end of our conversation, we had a web of all of their thinking about airplanes.

I no longer wondered about the nature of this play. It was apparent that we were beginning a real inquiry into airplanes; an airplane project was evolving. Once again, pretend play had become the provocation for meaningful literacy learning. I was ready to see where the play of paper airplanes would take us.

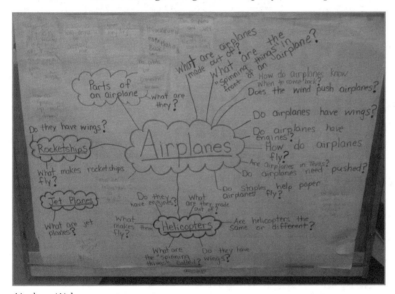

Airplane Web

The children's paper airplanes continued to present one major problem—they wouldn't fly! Of course they asked me for help. In this moment, I saw two choices, the easier being to make a paper airplane for them so they could all copy my model. But, I thought to myself, where is the learning in that? Instead, as I listened to the children, I recalled the bug project and how important talk had been in that inquiry. Therefore, I encouraged the students to work together to figure out the paper airplane problem independently. In addition, I filled the room with books about airplanes to help provide guidance in solving their problem. The airplane project overflowed into readers workshop.

Research in Kindergarten Workshop

Books became a new resource as the class continued to construct paper airplanes. During readers workshop, we read different nonfiction books together, including *Helicopters* by Jeffrey Zuehlke, *Airplanes* by Darlene Stille, *How People Learned to Fly* by Fran Hodgkins, and *If You Were A . . . Pilot* by Virginia Schomp. We revisited and revised the chart paper web with new information and lots of new questions. I encouraged the children to use Post-it notes as they read to jot down answers to questions on our web. Working, talking, and reading together, the students filled up sticky notes with information about their questions. Soon, Post-it notes were everywhere!

As I observed the children pursuing this inquiry, I noticed that two questions kept coming up: "What are the parts of an airplane?" and "How do airplanes fly?" To support the students' interest and curiosity, I read part of a book titled *Airplanes* by Hal Rogers. In response to this book, many of the kids cre-

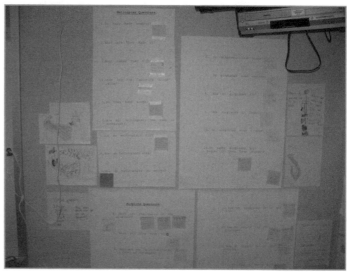

Sticky Note Research

ated pictures of planes as a way to sort out and represent their new understandings. We posted these on a large class collaborative mural under the question, "What are the parts of an airplane?"

At the same time, airplane books were becoming popular constructions during writers workshop. In these artifacts, the children explored the idea of how planes fly as well as how the parts of an airplane work. This is where all the information seemed to come together for the children. Their airplane play provoked questions, which led to research, which in turn led them to document their hypotheses about airplanes in pictures and words. Project work had once again merged with both readers and writers workshop through play.

In the midst of conducting research and writing about airplanes, the children were also collaboratively constructing an airport in the block area. This new round of play provided more opportunities for talk, reading, and writing as the students created labels for each part of the airport. Both oral and written vocabularies were developing through this project.

After about a week of reading and writing about airports, the children wanted to build another one; they had learned new things and wanted to represent the changes in their learning.

Labeling the Airport

CHILD 1: This can be where they get gas.

CHILD 2: We are using teamwork and working together!

CHILD 3: We need to make more airplanes for our airport!

CHILD 4: Airplane alert! That means that the airplane is out of gas and needs to go get some more!

CHILD 5: Here is where they go.

CHILD 1: These airplanes are parking here because there are no more people.

CHILD 2: More people will come to the airport tomorrow.

CHILD 4: We need to build this wall higher.

The new airport looked nothing like the first one! This time the children's focus was on making a parking garage for the airplanes and a place where they could get gas. Even though a great deal of planning went into this, soon they wanted to take this second airport down and build again. The more they learned about the parts of an airport and how it worked, the more they wanted to make new airports to show what they knew. In my observations and noting taking of students' conversations, I noticed many of the children using the vocabulary they had gained during their research and that now flooded the room in class charts, webs, and other written artifacts. The labels on the airport were another example of written language children used to show their learning. They were demonstrating meaning making through block constructions as they used these objects to represent the ideas they were learning through their reading and research. This kind of fantasy play gave them ample opportunity to practice separating objects from ideas through representation.

As the building of airports continued, the children decided that we needed airplanes that were not made of paper.

CHILD 1: "We need to make airplanes out of wood!"

This effort became the next step in our learning process. We wrote a letter as a class to our families asking for wood and other supplies for our airplanes. We organized teams to plan this process: two teams would sand the wood and get all the supplies ready; two teams would do the construction, actually putting the airplanes together; and the final two teams were in charge of painting the airplanes after they were built.

All of this work organizing teams and materials gave children even more opportunity for relevant talk and social interaction to support their literacy learning. As in the bug project, the creation of representations functioned like symbolic play; wood was used to represent an airplane, just as earlier the blocks represented an airport. The ability to use objects to represent other things for a specific purpose was practice for the children in understanding that words can also represent "things" in their environment.

The students' final quest in the airplane project developed when the children decided that we needed to make an airport that could be saved forever. We had already made a lot of airports out of the blocks in our room, but these could never be permanent. The children wanted to make a 3-D representation of an airport that could be saved forever. So we began collecting old shoe boxes, toilet paper rolls, and small cardboard boxes to help with this process.

In about a week, the children were ready to build their airport. Using what we had learned from our reading in readers workshop, we first made a list of the different parts of the airport that we would construct. These were the Jetway, bathroom, control tower, parents' room, game room, game store, candy store, food court, baggage claim, and check-in counter. Then each child chose one part of the airport to work on, with two people on each team for each part of our airport. The first mission of each team was to draw a plan of exactly what they wanted their part of the airport to look like. After this plan was finished, the building began. After two weeks of hard work, the children were finished and we put all the pieces together. At last the children had finished their airplane research.

The cardboard airport, our culminating project, sat on a very special shelf in our room, a daily reminder to all of us of the hard work and learning that happened during our airplane project. Once again, as in the bug project, children's learning was authentic, meaningful, and full of literacy experiences. In both projects, children were inspired by play that then served as an essential provocation for learning, providing energy that pushed our inquiries effectively into readers and writers workshops.

My work as a teacher-researcher, particularly the ongoing close observations of children and documentation of their talk, helped me build a detailed, data-based image of children as capable, curious, and active; to stay connected with their inquiry; and to see the relationships they were building (see Figure 2.1). Teacher research enabled me to keep track of their learning and respond thoughtfully as the students reconstructed and integrated the curricular structures of project work and workshop through play.

What I Learned

Through this study, I learned a great deal about how children's play influences inquiry and the project work that grows from it, as well as how it can fuel both readers and writers workshop in authentic ways. In our bug project, children's play led them to many literacy opportunities. Content-rich talk permeated their play, affording many possibilities for oral vocabulary development. As part of this play, the children were also continually using different objects to represent something else, thereby practicing a concept foundational to literacy: one thing can stand for another, like letters for sounds. Of course, the students also had lots of experiences with written language: wide reading of nonfiction, construction of class webs and charts, labeling mailboxes and block buildings, writing the Bug Food Restaurant menu and ABC chart, and endless writers workshop little books.

My study supports the idea that play can be viewed as what our Italian colleagues in Reggio Emilia call a "provocation"—something that inspires learning. Playing with insects, building with blocks, creating the Bug Food Restaurant, and making paper airplanes led to more learning than I could ever have imagined. In addition, this study shows that play can be a way in which children meaningfully integrate the curricular structures of classroom life, in this case project work and readers and writers workshops.

Data Source	Data	What Relationships?	Interpretation	Curricular Decision	Research Decision
Children's Talk	Talk about the bug restaurant	Child to Curriculum	Children are using fantasy play and talk to extend their inquiry from bugs to restaurants.	Provide time and guidance for the creation of the bug menu.	Watch for further extensions of inquiry, make note of fantasy, photograph written artifacts, type up children's talk.
Written Artifacts	Bug ABC chart	Child to Curriculum and to Subject of Literacy	Children are merging their project work with the tools used in workshop.	• Allow flexibility; follow children's lead. • Provide materials and guidance for ABC chart construction.	Note interest in extending project into workshop through materials, photographs, written artifacts; type up children's talk.
Children's Talk	"How do you make a paper airplane?"	Child to Materials and Child to Subject of Airplanes	Using talk to investigate an idea.	• Provide time, space, and materials for further talk and experimentation with paper. • Provide books to support new inquiry.	Document talk and photograph exploration of materials; record titles of books.
Written Artifacts	Notes to bugs	Child to Curriculum	Children using fantasy to extend project, resulting in merger of workshop with project work.	• Encourage note writing as new genre; follow children's lead in constructing mailboxes. • Continue to provide time, space, and materials for play.	Document talk and photograph artifacts; make note of use of fantasy play.
Photographs	Pictures of block constructions of airport	Child to Materials and to Curriculum and Subject of Airplanes	Children using building to make sense of new information.	• Continue to provide time, space, and materials to explore idea of airplanes and airports. • See if a visit to the airport is possible.	Document talk and photograph constructions regularly; note use of materials to investigate ideas learned through reading.

Note: Children's relationships with one another are a part of all their work. Here I tried to highlight other kinds of relationships.

Figure 2.1. Relationality chart for Amanda's classroom.

Flaxman (2000) tells us that "[p]lay is a necessary part of growing up" (p. 39). For me it is also a necessary part of classroom life, particularly one in which the child is seen as a capable and competent inquirer. Play is also an essential component in transforming children into literate beings. As Owocki (1999) says, "Play is like a gold mine in its potential for facilitating literacy" (p. 3). This gold mine should be mined daily in all early childhood classrooms to promote meaningful literacy across the day for children. Play is not just important; it is essential.

Bibliography

Chard, S. C. (1994). *The project approach: Making curriculum come alive*. New York: Scholastic.

Da Ros-Voseles, D., Danyi, D., & Aurillo, J. (2003). Aligning professional preparation and practice: Bringing constructivist learning to kindergarten. *Dimensions of Early Childhood, 31*(2), 33–38.

Flaxman, S. G. (2000). Play, an endangered species. *Instructor, 110*(2), 39.

Hankins, K. H. (2003). *Teaching through the storm: A journal of hope*. New York: Teachers College Press.

Hatch, J. A. (2005). *Teaching in the new kindergarten*. Clifton Park, NY: Thomson Delmar Learning.

Owocki, G. (1999). *Literacy through play*. Portsmouth, NH: Heinemann.

Children's Literature Cited

Barner, B. (1999). *Bugs, bugs, bugs!*. San Francisco: Chronicle Books.

Hodgkins, F. (2007). *How people learned to fly*. New York: HarperCollins.

Llewellyn, C. (1998). *The best book of bugs*. New York: Kingfisher.

Parker, J. (1997). *I love spiders*. New York: Scholastic.

Parker, N. W., & Wright, J. R. (1988). *Bugs*. New York: Mulberry Books.

Rogers, H. (2001). *Airplanes*. Chanhassen, MN: Child's World.

Schomp, V. (1999). *If you were a . . . pilot*. New York: Benchmark Books.

Sill, C. (2003). *About insects: A guide for children*. Atlanta: Peachtree.

Stille, D. (1997). *Airplanes*. New York: Children's Press.

Zuehlke, J. (2005). *Helicopters*. Minneapolis: Lerner.

◉ Research Conversations: Focusing on Classroom Talk

WITH AMANDA ANGLE

JUDY: As you know, I am talking about how all the teacher-researchers in our group have developed an interest in one particular kind of research strategy in the course of their work. When I was looking at your work, it struck me that keeping track of children's talk and really looking at their language was an important part of your study. Can you talk a little bit about the history of that, how you came to do that?

AMANDA: When I taught preschool, I taught threes and fours. I was really trying to encourage my threes to talk. I found myself taking pictures of their play and other things they were doing and hanging their pictures up in the room or putting their pictures in binders so they could look at them. I hoped it would start [them] talking, to really get them forming sentences and developing their oral language.

JUDY: And using the children's own experience as a provocation for talk makes sense.

AMANDA: Yes, they loved it. They were very interested. Of course, my four-year-olds were already talking some. But I still sat and listened to them talk. I wrote down their conversations when they played and then read those conversations back to them. It would get them talking and remembering what they [had done] and even get them talking *more* about their experiences. When I came back to kindergarten, I realized how important that was and thought if it was important with threes and fours, it's going to be even more important with fives.

JUDY: It seems that one of the things you learned with your preschool group was that in revisiting their play in the talk you recorded in writing and in photographs, not only did they remember things but the documentation served as a provocation for further thinking. Whereas maybe they would have dropped what they were thinking about, what they were talking about, if you hadn't done this. Talk a little bit about how you started to take down children's talk in your kindergarten classroom.

AMANDA: I would sit with a group of children during free choice time, usually in the block area, sometimes in other places, but usually in blocks.

JUDY: So you did this during free choice time? How about project time?

AMANDA: Well, our project work would happen during free choice time. Usually whatever project we were doing, they would naturally "play" that in free choice time.

JUDY: So this was a natural overlap that the children created.

AMANDA: Absolutely. So I would sit there with my notebook and my camera and I would write down what the children were saying. I would never get concerned about who was saying what. I was just concerned with the conversation going on and what was happening, and having the pictures to go with the dialogue. If I felt it would be useful or if it was a great scenario, I would type up the talk that I wrote down and insert the pictures with them and make a book. The next day before free choice time, we would revisit their play by reading the book together, and it would provoke more play during [free] choice time that day.

JUDY: So you used the book you created from observing their play as a shared reading?

AMANDA: Yes.

JUDY: In your study, "Project Work Meets Workshop," you refer to Child 1, Child 2, and Child 3. You don't use names. I guess that this is an artifact of you watching the *group* rather than one individual. This seems important. In American culture we focus so much on the individual; how that individual does lots of things, that individual's test scores and benchmarks and all that. So this is like one of those times where you really see how a group is doing and how a group is helping each [child] think together, play together, pursue a project or ideas together.

AMANDA: Yes. And I would always write down the [names of the] group of children that was there just in case they weren't captured in a photo. It was interesting to see if the group grew over time; what was the common thread? Who was the leader? If one of the leaders was absent, sometimes the group would be smaller. It was interesting to see the patterns over time, just by writing down who was playing but not really worrying about who was saying what.

JUDY: It's so apparent in your study that the *social interactions*, particularly the play of children, drove the project and helped them make these links across the curriculum. They brought play into project [time] and workshop. They moved things around through the social interaction, so it makes sense that the group interaction was important for you to focus on. Can you describe just physically how you recorded children's talk?

AMANDA: I had a three-ring binder and I would just very informally, and not very neatly, write down what they said. Well, you know, they talk really fast! But two or three times a week I would go to the computer and type up my notes. I didn't type up every conversation I wrote down. But at least two or three times a week, I would go to my computer. I put it all in one document so that it ended up being a timeline of the progression of our project in pictures and in dialogue.

JUDY: Did you date the entries?

AMANDA: I dated every conversation in my notebook, but not on the computer, because it was more the evolution I was interested in.

JUDY: But in your notebook?

AMANDA: In my notebook I would date the conversation and write the names of all the kids I was observing at the top of the page.

JUDY: Did you try to get their actual words?

AMANDA: Yes, their direct language, even if it was not Standard English or grammatically correct. I wrote what the children said verbatim.

JUDY: So let me go back to the computer. You had everything in one file and you uploaded the pictures from your camera.

AMANDA: Yes, I took the pictures that matched the dialogue and inserted them in a Word document.

JUDY: It seems like in doing this that you also got a chance to revisit the learning that happened, and you probably noticed things you hadn't noticed even though you were right there taking down the conversation.

AMANDA: Yes, and it helped me when I created the documentation panels that everything was in chronological order. I could just cut and paste the important aspects of the children's work into a PowerPoint, which is what I use to create the panels.

JUDY: You know, Amanda, as you talk it makes me think about what the Reggio educators call the "pedagogy of listening." I wonder if you could talk a bit about how this put you in touch with the kids as opposed to if you were just going through a structured curriculum.

AMANDA: Taking the time to actually sit and listen is so important in getting to know your kids. In the past five years, since there are more and more things coming down from higher up that we *have to* do, [. . .] I've seen my playtime shrink. But I really make a point to take at least thirty minutes a day to just sit and listen. I have a black comfortable chair in my room that is right by where most of [the kids] play, and I just sit there and watch and write down their conversations. Of course, you don't write down conversations every day. It may be one day you have someone on your lap telling you about what they did last night or what they're going to do this weekend. But the relationships that you build and things that you learn are just amazing. If you don't take the time to do this, if you're always pulling small groups so they can learn their letters or some other skill, you never have these relationships. So I just make it a point that thirty minutes of every day I am just going to sit and listen or have a conversation. It's just like you do when you go to the coffeehouse with your friends, just a conversation about life. Because if you don't know the children, you can't really reach them academically anyway.

JUDY: So it's almost like a relational investment in the children. An investment that you want to make both because you're a human being and you want to know who they are and also because in the end it helps you instruct them in even the most discrete things like you suggested, like learning their letters.

AMANDA: Right. And it just lets them know that you care. They're only five and six years old. They need to know that you really care about them. I feel like once they realize that, then they talk to you all the time during the day. So you can sit with them and conference about their writing in writers workshop, but at the same time they're telling you lots of other things about themselves—because you have that kind of relationship.

JUDY: So even in workshop you end up learning more about them because of the listening you've done earlier. I wonder if that even promotes a different kind of writing. They are talking to you more, which is giving them all kinds of oral language practice, which we all know helps them in their writing. But they're also maybe more willing to talk about a wider variety of things with someone who really cares about them. I would imagine that would help generate ideas.

AMANDA: Yes, and I feel that there is just so much now going on with accountability, and it's not that I don't think we should be accountable. We should be. But one of the things that happens is that school is more pressured and there is the pressure to move—BOOM, BOOM, BOOM— through the day. I feel that the children need to know that I am their teacher, that I am going to take the time to sit and talk with them, joke around, and play.

JUDY: Ms. Angle is going to pay attention to us.

AMANDA: I have heard many of my colleagues in the past few years get really frustrated during choice or playtime because they think it's just this crazy, chaotic time when the kids are just running around and chasing each other. Sometimes I wonder what *they* are doing during that time. I know that if I sit at [my] computer or [am] busy with something, the children start thinking, what's the point of what I am doing right now?

JUDY: So you validate the activity of play for them.

AMANDA: Yes, and they are engaged and purposeful in their interactions.

JUDY: This is one of the things we've talked about in our teacher research group, the idea that the data collection process actually benefits children. It reminds me, of course, of the Reggio educators, who believe that when we observe children, they come to know how important they are. Observing is a way of honoring them. You're observing them because it's interesting, because you're curious, because you want to know them. You care about them.

AMANDA: I want them to play and interact with each other nicely on a daily basis. I don't want them to do it when I just happen to be sitting and watching them. I want it to be a natural thing for them.

JUDY: It also seems from your work that that regular time for play is what allows them to bring their other work into play, like their project work and their readers and writers workshop books.

AMANDA: Yes, and you wonder what their play would look like if they didn't have large blocks of time to play regularly.

JUDY: You wonder if they would develop these cross-curricular connections, or a sustained interest in something. The Reggio educators talk a lot about the use of space and time, and it occurs to me that what you are doing with your observation and taking down children's talk, with your listening, is that you are creating space and time for children to use play to make sense of a lot of what goes on in school and what goes on in their worlds.

AMANDA: Yes, most recently they are playing "city bus." I don't know if someone has been on a bus recently, but they'll set all the chairs up in lines and rows. Somebody's the driver and they've got the blocks for the pedals. When you ask them where they're going, some of them are going to the mall and they've all got tickets. Someone in the group knows the procedures. It's a bus that has seatbelts, because they all have blocks on their laps for seatbelts. Whether it's classroom things or things in the world, it is their time to figure out this crazy world.

JUDY: They have time to sustain an interest, like this exploration of the city bus or in the work you did in the bug project, where they continually built in the block area these bug cities. If they didn't have regular time, what would that work have looked like?

Well, Amanda, I wonder if you have any tips for teachers, something you might tell people interested in doing this kind of observation and documentation as a part of teacher research work.

AMANDA: I would just say that if you skip out on doing the observations, the listening, and the noticing of children's talk, it's going to hurt you in the long run, especially in terms of community. I'll never forget my first year of teaching. I had a tough group. They were great individual kids, but they had so much trouble being together. I remember, with the help of colleagues I spent a couple of months integrating all my literacy work with building community. Had I not spent the time doing that I really don't think there would have been much learning that year. If you don't take the time to sit and listen, know your kids, and build trust, those academic skills are never going to happen. The kids that I am working with now don't have a lot of adults in their lives that they can trust. It takes a long time to build that trust, longer than any of us would like. But if you don't build that trust, they're not going to get their letters or numbers and they're not going to care. If you don't show them that you care, why should they care?

JUDY: Observation, listening, and creating documentation as a part of your day lets them know you care.

AMANDA: Yes.

JUDY: Well, that sounds like a great place to stop. Thank you, Amanda.

Building Identity as a Language Learner: How Reggio Foundations Inspired Workshop Flexibility

3

KAREN K. GOLDSTEIN

I hope that all teachers, at least once at some point in their careers, are privileged to have an experience that is so profound that they are changed forever. This chapter reflects just such an experience for me; it is the story of one extraordinary child from whom I was privileged to learn. Eric made such a difference in how I think about teaching and learning, what I know about children, and how I view my role as a teacher that I ended the school year as an entirely different person, wholly transformed through my relationship with him.

This chapter tells part of Eric's story—a remarkable journey of an English language learner making his way through his kindergarten year in a mostly monolingual public school classroom. It is also a story about my inquiry and my journey of becoming a teacher-researcher, political advocate, and better teacher for *all* of my students.

The theme of building, which runs throughout my work, is extremely literal on the one hand and metaphorical on the other. Eric's first positive public attempts to enter our kindergarten community were a product of his success as an architect in the classroom Building Zone. On the metaphorical level are the myriad ways he and I and his classmates, sometimes together and sometimes individually, built connections, capacity, understandings, bridges, scaffolds, and friendships and made sense of what it means to become a literate participant in a democratic community—no matter who you are.

I suspect that if we truly value all our learners, listen carefully, and look closely at their many, many inquiries into making meaning of this existence, we'd find ourselves in the transcendent position of new understandings more often than we generally do. If I had to compress all of these experiences, all of these understandings into one thought, what I know now, and what has made me a better teacher—a better *person*— is that being different makes all the difference, and we're *all* different. Eric, like all his peers, was just as different as—and no different than—every other kid.

Our Context

On any given day, our kindergarten classroom bustles with the productive hum of busy five- and six-year-olds at work. As I look around the spacious, bright, well-provisioned full-day kindergarten classroom, I have to smile. It's March, and by this point in the year the diverse group of learners who inhabit this space is largely independent. Valerie, Augusto, Ernesto, and Lalan are working in the latest iteration of the Dramatic Play corner taking orders and baking pizza in the refrigerator-box-improvised "Pizza Place." In the meeting area, Ramona, Sarah, Aiden, and Accalia clamor around Brandon, the villainous wolf in a dramatic retelling of *The Three Little Pigs*. Maggie, seated in the rocking chair nearby, watches and claps delightedly as she and her assistant act as the audience. Livi and Monique read together intently on the futon under the loft, in spite of the peals of silly laughter and playful banter emanating from Peter, Neil, and Alonso, who are writing "love notes" in the Writing Center above them. Evan and Jaila are at the glass easel in the Art Center, concentrating on carefully mixing colors to paint a still life of spring tulips. Taylor, Susan, Ryan, and Angel are listening (again!) to a recording of Ray Charles singing "Chicka Chicka Boom Boom" in the Listening Center. Esmeralda and Daniela, pointers in hand, are roaming the classroom, excitedly pointing out all the words they know how to read. And, of course, Eric and Colin are ensconced in the Building Zone as usual, carefully adding to and rearranging their latest use-every-block-in-the-Building-Zone creation.

These eager learners have bloomed in the midst of our accepting, diverse community through a combination of carefully taught and practiced routines, with a strong emphasis on being members of a democratic community. The pressures of standardized tests and push-down curriculum haven't hit us with too much force just yet, so our days flow relatively free of the clock. We begin with a free choice time and continue with a community circle/morning meeting (Kriete, 2002), where the "strong arms of teaching" (Ray & Cleveland, 2004, p. 39) in the form of shared reading, repeated big book readings, and interactive writing (McCarrier, Pinell, & Fountas, 2000) wrap themselves around us. We continue with writers workshop (Ray & Cleveland, 2004; Calkins, 1994), and then lunch, a chapter book read-aloud, recess, and finally readers workshop (Calkins, 2001; Collins, 2004) and math workshop. Science and social studies are integrated throughout the day, usually by way of our current project (Katz & Chard, 2000) during free choice time. The children have many opportunities to choose the activities they engage in and with whom. At multiple times during the day, I work with individuals or small groups based on their needs as determined by my careful observations and notes.

My Study: Inquiring into Language Learning

Meeting Eric

Eric's family seemed no different from the six other families I had already met that August day. The kindergartners were lucky to start school a few days after the "big kids," and they and their families came in for individual family meetings with their teachers. Eric and his parents arrived at the classroom door at their appointed time, peering in nervously. I looked to make eye contact with my student first and spotted Eric standing shyly behind his mom, who was standing slightly behind his dad. I greeted them enthusiastically and invited them with words and a gesture to come into the room and have a seat at the large round table in the center. They stood by the table somewhat uncomfortably, and I began talking—trying to break the ice, build some rapport. A nervous silence ensued. I froze, realizing there must be an issue with my language. "Would it help if I found someone to help us?" I stammered, pointing at the door. Eric's father smiled uncomfortably and nodded yes. I wasn't sure if he knew what I had said, or if it was my gestures and the complete look of panic on my face that explained, but I raised my finger and said, "Just a minute." I walked out of the room and then ran down the hall to find our English for Speakers of Other Languages (ESOL) teacher.

In my fifteen years of teaching, in spite of working in a district with a growing Latino population, I had never taught a student who did not speak English. I realized, with the immediacy of "Oh my gosh! I have to do this right-this-very-minute!," that I was about to embark on a new direction in my teaching and learning. I had no idea what I should do, what to expect, or even where to start to build a relationship with and include and instruct this child—and his six other classmates whom I soon discovered had all indicated that a language other than English was spoken at home.

That year I struggled to make sense of the children in my room. The immediate moment-to-moment needs and frustrations of these learners remained largely a mystery to me. What finally helped me gain some insight came from a town in Italy and a curricular structure popularized by Teachers College in New York City. It seems unlikely that two such disparate influences could have led to such profound understandings, but that is exactly how it unfolded.

Data Generation

Throughout the school year, I carefully observed and documented Eric's and his classmates' growth and development as literate beings in my room. I began by taking many photographs and keeping daily anecdotal notes, written on a page of standard-sized mailing labels. (See the appendix at the end of this chapter for my record-keeping process.) I carried my clipboard around with me and recorded my observations, very informally, especially during our workshops and free choice time.

I recorded almost everything I noticed about my learners, from their behaviors, to what they specifically wrote during writers workshop, to the books they were reading during readers workshop, to the specific teaching point of my individual conferences. I then collected the labels in a small binder tabbed with a page for each child. Usually at the end of the day, I took just a few minutes as I put the labels in the binder to jot down any other things I remembered, and more often than not, those quick writing notes turned into much longer observations that often surprised me by leading me to new understandings about what the kids were actually up to during the day. Two or three times a week—or as interesting events occurred—I wrote for more extended periods in my research journal. I also saved or photocopied children's work when I found it particularly interesting, exciting, or perplexing.

As the year progressed, I celebrated our successes, grew frustrated at my inadequacy, and took my notes and photographs to our study group to help me make sense of what was happening so that I could improve my practice. Throughout the year I studied my notes, matched them as well as my research journal writing to the relevant pieces of student work, and used my colleagues' collective wisdom to help me identify just what it was that I wondered and to look for patterns in my data. I pored over photographs and hypothesized about what children were doing and why, and then went back into my classroom to observe some more and either confirm or disconfirm my ideas.

Eric's Story: Inquiring into Language

In spite of seemingly insurmountable language challenges, I decided I really couldn't do anything but make the best of the situation and proceed as I always did. As the school year began, I jumped into my usual routines for building community. The students and I read wonderful picture books together; sang songs; compared, cheered, and chanted one anothers' names; and shared stories from home. Most of the children in my class responded enthusiastically in ways I expected. I hooked them on books such as Bill Martin and John Archambault's *Chicka, Chicka, Boom Boom*, Bill Martin's *Brown Bear, Brown Bear, What Do You See?*, and Alexis O'Neill's *The Recess Queen* and had them begging to sing "Tony

Chestnut" or "Head, Shoulders, Knees, and Toes" just one more time. They took quickly and happily to "making stuff" (Ray & Cleveland, 2004, p. 6) that resembled books and spending significant chunks of time engaged with books during our readers and writers workshops.

Eric, however, was a different story. He would not join our whole-group activities and sat at the table in the Dramatic Play center with his head down or under one of the other tables, stubbornly refusing to join in anything we did as a group. His attempts during writers workshop, when he would make them—usually only with an adult nearby—resembled those of a much younger child, and he would only spend time with books if an adult was sitting with him. His behavior puzzled and concerned me. I couldn't imagine why he wouldn't want to be with his classmates. I could not understand why he didn't find our fun songs and books as entertaining as his friends did. I now realize that he couldn't picture himself as a part of these activities—and how could he? He didn't know what I said as I read books or why we moved in all sorts of silly ways as we sang. I can only imagine how alienating the classroom must have felt to Eric.

After a month or more of sitting in the Dramatic Play corner not participating, Eric finally found a way in. On September 2, I wrote in my anecdotal notes:

> He's into touching and just giggling hysterically at people—not a good thing! Not sure how to improve that, but he is beginning to say things in English—he and Augusto were saying "PUSH!" to each other as they pushed in line.

Eric's choice for entering our community was as a detractor. He sat at the back of the group and either talked nonstop in Spanish to one of the other Spanish-speaking children, cackled loudly when no one else was laughing, or poked and bothered some other child, usually an English-speaking one. He had found a way into our community—but as a "bad boy" (Gallas, 1997). Only by acting out could he show any control over the foreign situation of an English-speaking classroom. Still, it was something of a relief that Eric was at least *trying* to join the community. I just needed to figure out how to help him find a more productive way in. During the first semester, in spite of—or maybe because of—my utter lack of experience and knowledge about teaching children whose first language is different from my own, I did not observe Eric as carefully as I did later. I did know that he eventually seemed to be adjusting to our ways of being and doing. He played with other children in the classroom and especially on the playground. I realized much later, however, after I became involved with my study group and began analyzing my anecdotal notes, that he *had* been a huge presence in the Building Zone from very early in the year, working to hone his meaning making through block building. I found that in December I had noticed that he was building in the Building Zone often, and that his buildings were highly unusual. From my anecdotal notes:

> Eric 12/7—Very into the building zone and quite productive.
> How can I use that to my advantage?

I also noted that he was able to direct other children to assist him, not only in building but also in doing other routine classroom jobs like signing his name each morning. In fact, he was the catalyst for a huge reorganization of the classroom in December, which inadvertently resulted in the creation of time and space for me to really tune into the inquiries he was making about this new language into which he'd been thrown. I later realized that Eric absolutely *was* participating all along; I just hadn't noticed or valued his inquiries as legitimate literate practices in our classroom.

Building with Blocks as "Authoring" during Writers Workshop

The big "Aha!" for me—and as it turned out for Eric as well, because *I* finally recognized it—came in February. I later realized by looking through the many pictures I had taken over the year that as a five-year-old architect, Eric built distinctive buildings. They were tall, linear, and symmetrical. In the range of "typical" kindergarten buildings I had observed, Eric's were unusual. Often he and the two or three other children working with him would use every single one of the wooden blocks in our extensive set to complete the construction. The Building Zone began the year under our loft. But by December, the constructions had become so complex and massive that this space was too constraining. After a class meeting, a unanimous decision was made to move the Building Zone across the room to the site of the classroom Library and to put the Library under the loft. This created significantly more width as well as height in which to build—and Eric took full advantage of the extra space.

One day in February during writers workshop, I sat conferring on the carpet with a group of writers. Ever vigilant about what was going on in the classroom, I was suddenly distracted by the clank of blocks in the Building Zone. "Hey!" I thought. "That's not okay; it's writing time!" I walked over to that part of the classroom to find Eric, entrenched in his familiar spot, repairing part of his building.

My initial instinct was to say, "Eric, go back to your table and get busy on your writing!," but for some reason I stopped for a moment to really watch what he was up to. What I saw absolutely floored me. Eric wasn't just fixing his building in a blatant disregard of our classroom expectations; he was drawing detailed plans of his architecture so that he could reproduce the buildings if they should get knocked down. My developing image of the child as protagonist in his own learning must have reached a tipping point that allowed me to view Eric's work differently and revalue the amazing "text" he was creating.

I think this was the moment of an important shift for me. I suddenly realized that Eric wasn't being "bad" or defying me; he was "authoring" his way into our curriculum in a way that made the most sense to him. My research question had finally become fully formed: *In what ways is Eric inquiring into the English language, and how can I support his inquiries?*

Building Relationships with Texts and More Conventional Skills in Readers and Writers Workshops

That singular recognition of Eric's competence in the Building Zone led to what seemed at the time like a rush of literacy inquiries for him. In hindsight, looking through my notes, I can see that Eric had been slowly building understandings all along. He could find his friends' names from our interactive word wall when he wanted to write them, he would identify animals in books and objects in the classroom by their English names, and he often pointed out letters on the computer keyboard that were in his or his friends' names. As a class, we had a

Eric's Architectural Plans

number of "touchstone" texts that we read from the beginning of the year and came back to frequently. As Eric's literacy skills grew, these texts became the springboards for his attempts to create his own books during writers workshop. He was especially drawn to books written or illustrated by Eric Carle, possibly because he delighted in recognizing his own name on each book! He made versions of *Brown Bear, Brown Bear, What Do You See?* (Martin), *Panda Bear, Panda Bear, What Do You See?* (Martin), and *Mister Seahorse* (Carle), often just copying some of the words onto his own pages. He also loved *No, David!*, *David Goes to School*, and *David Gets in Trouble* by David Shannon. In a joyous glimpse of his clever sense of humor, he proudly wrote his own version of *No, David!* about one of his more rambunctious classmates titled "No Eduardo!"

Like many of his peers, Eric wrote books inspired by the television shows and movies he saw: Spider-Man, Scooby-Doo, Shrek, and Dora the Explorer. He also wrote "bed-to-bed" stories that narrated all the events of his day, using words he had learned to spell independently such as *school, snack,* and *home,* as well as words he could find in the classroom.

The work Eric did during writers workshop began to overlap his work during readers workshop, and the more he learned the more he sought me out to be a co-constructor. I worked to find simple emergent texts in both English and Spanish for him to put in his individual reading bag, and we read them together often to increase *both* of our language skills. One February day, Eric stayed after school. I captured the experience in my notes:

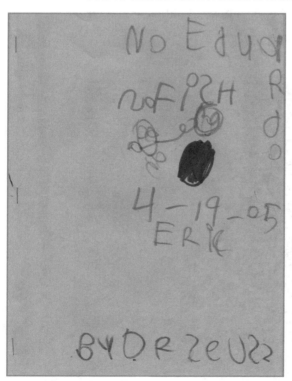

Eric's Version of No, David!

He wanted to look at *No David*—he read me the cover and first page! ☺ Very proud! I wonder if he has it at home? He kinda walked away, but would come back to look at each page as I read. On the "Go to your room!" page, I said, to him "Ah—tu cuarto, si?" connecting to the book *Mi Cuarto* in his RW bag—he went and got it, and I read it—he is sooo obviously wanting to make these text connections—it's amazing!

These sorts of text-to-text connections began to happen more and more frequently for Eric as he started to cement his membership in our literacy club (Smith, 1988).

One of Eric's most poignant literacy moments came on a spring day during readers workshop. I had deliberately chosen a simple question book with repetitive text from our Rigby series called *Where Is Eric?* by Anne Bauers because it had his name in it and I imagined that the connection to his name would provide him with an instant connection to the book. He was happy to read it with me, and we worked on the English vocabulary for all the places in the

Making Connections

story the boy and mother look to find a missing dog. As the story culminates, the second to last page says, "Look . . ." and then on the final page, "here he is!" as they successfully find the dog. I evaluated the conference as a successful literacy experience—Eric seemed to relate to the text, I felt like he had added some new words to his repertoire, and I was doing my job well.

But Eric wasn't finished with the book that easily. Later in the day he came to get me because he wanted to show me something. He had noticed a magnet hanging on my file cabinet that simply said, "Look." He excitedly pointed to it and said what I heard as "perdo." I asked him to repeat it and still heard "perdo," which puzzled me. *Perdo* was not a word I recognized. As always seems to happen at school, we ran out of time to figure out what he was saying that day, but the next day he came back to it. I got out my Spanish–English dictionary and we both kept trying to solve our language puzzle. After several attempts to figure out what connection he was making, *Where Is Eric?* came to my mind. It finally occurred to me that Eric must be saying *perro*—the word for "dog" in Spanish. He had assumed that the page with "Look . . ." on it referred to the dog, and the magnet must therefore mean the same thing. I was floored by his brilliant observation and marveled at just how far this once seemingly unresponsive English language learner had come.

Building Capacity for Relational Work

At the same time Eric was making connections to and between texts, he was also a protagonist in our ongoing class project. As with so much of what happened

Sign Making

that year, I realized only later that his presence during our project time had a significant influence on how the project played out, as well as helped him to build capacity for all of the other work in which he engaged. One important aspect of our classroom that contributed to Eric's involvement in this part of our day was a shared culture of sign making. For whatever reason, perhaps motivated by an earlier "label the room" activity for our parents' visit on Back-to-School Night, this particular group of children had developed as a community of sign makers. The children labeled almost everything they could in the classroom, making signs cautioning people not to run in the school, reminding them to sign in if they wanted to be the "Boss" of the Building Zone, and warning them not to knock down buildings. This particular project began when my student teacher and I noticed that a number of children (including Eric) were often playing "restaurant" in the Dramatic Play area.

Making the Pizza Car

We seeded the space with menus, small notepads for taking orders, a telephone, and some aprons. The restaurant play continued and often seemed to be about pizza. We had some class discussions about what the children knew about pizza, and I decided to see what would happen if I brought in a refrigerator box to add to the Dramatic Play area. Much discussion ensued about the box, and the students first decided that it should be a pizza car to deliver the pizza.

After several incidents in which many children piled into the car and strained the integrity of the cardboard box, the kids decided to limit the number of children who could be in the box at any one time to just four. Signs were quickly made to let everyone know how many children could be in the car, but Eric, for some reason, disagreed. Even as his friends put signs with "4" on the side of the pizza car, Eric stubbornly put his own sign on the box saying that "5" could go in.

Signs for Car Occupancy

The pizza play continued. The children fashioned pizzas from many different materials and even made their own real pizza, slicing pepperoni, blending homemade sauce, and grating cheese. Our study continued with a visit to a local pizza restaurant, where we toured the kitchen and watched pizzas being made. That visit spurred even more inventive play, and the pizza car turned into a pizza store complete with ATM machine!

At all points along the project, Eric was involved, making his own signs for the car and store, directing who could play and what they should do, and writing about pizza during writers workshop. It wasn't until the very end of the year that I learned just how criti- cal this pizza play was for Eric's aca-

The Pizza Store

demic success—his father worked in a pizza restaurant, and on the days he did not come to school, Eric spent his time there with his father. Pizza was a topic he knew well, and this unwitting home–school connection gave Eric an opportunity to feel confident in his school activities, even when reading and writing seemed elusive.

Building Gifts

As the year came to a close, though worried about sending Eric off to a first grade with more traditional expectations, I knew he was on his way. He had demonstrated in numerous different ways that he had many skills and tools with which to make sense of his world—all he needed was a responsive teacher to recognize them and provide appropriate scaffolds. I felt an immense sense of accomplishment in making so much progress with this child (and his classmates) who began as such a mystery to me. My greatest sense of accomplishment was recognizing that *I* had learned perhaps even more than Eric, and that I had expanded my understanding of what children can and will do if given the opportunity.

Eric, however, wasn't quite finished. On the last full day of school, he built

Literacy Touchstones

yet another use-every-block-in-the-classroom construction, perhaps more elaborate than ever before. But this one was special: intertwined throughout the tall columns were books—not just any books, but the touchstones that had been part of our shared experience: *Brown Bear, Brown Bear, What Do You See?* (Martin), *Chicka, Chicka, Boom Boom* (Martin & Archambault), *Duck on a Bike* (Shannon), *David Gets in Trouble* (Shannon), and, of course, *The Very Hungry Caterpillar*—because it was written by *Eric* Carle!

As I think about that afternoon several years later, I am still moved to tears. The wisdom of this one young child is stunning, as is his ability to communicate the power of these blocks and texts in a place where he was afforded the time and opportunity to find his *own* way to make sense of them. I know Eric will be successful in life, and I only hope that as a teacher

I can continue to rise to the challenge of helping *every* child find his or her way to becoming a full-fledged member of the literacy club.

Concluding Thoughts: Teacher as Researcher and a Pedagogy of Listening

Many factors allowed me to step back from my knowledge and comfort as a kindergarten teacher to follow Eric's lead in my classroom. Most important was the support of our dynamic and wise study group. But the ideas of the Reggio approach and the readers and writers workshop models also afforded me new lenses through which to consider my students' literacy development. My identification with Reggio philosophy facilitated my ability to stand back and figure out how my English learners were trying to join *us*, rather than mindlessly attempt to impose my ways of learning and involvement on them.

To make clear the connections between Reggio ideas and workshop structures, here are some of the issues and questions that arose—and that I pondered with my study group, framed by the ideas discussed in Chapter 2.

Image of the Child /Envisioning

As I worked with students who did not speak my language, I wondered: Do the practices and activities in my classroom reflect a strong, rich, competent image of a child for *them*? Does the environment I have prepared and am co-constructing with my learners reflect that image for *all* of them? Do I allow *all* of my students adequate time, space, and materials to be the protagonists in their own meaning making? Examining my practices in light of Reggio's image of the child caused a dramatic shift in my image of myself as a teacher.

Image of the Teacher

I realized that teacher research was the vehicle that allowed me to pursue my own classroom inquiries, not with the intent of "proving" some level of mastery or "fixing" some deficiency, but to genuinely make better sense of what I see happening in my classroom on a daily basis and to provide me with interpretations and directions for my ongoing work. As I worked with Eric, I wondered how teacher research might empower me to become an authoritative advocate for *all* of my students, and in what ways the image of a competent, inquiring teacher could contribute to the image of the teacher as an expert in the larger educational community. Viewing myself as a protagonist and co-constructor of curriculum afforded me the confidence and authority to document my work and validate my inquiries as well as the children's as essential to furthering our work in the classroom.

Documentation as Teacher Research and Inquiry as a Stance toward Teaching and Learning

As a protagonist in his own learning, Eric was a natural inquirer. For me as his teacher, noticing and naming these inquiries was fundamental to nurturing them and scaffolding further learning experiences for Eric and his classmates. Documenting student work through photographs and transcriptions of their conversations and ideas and then further reflecting on the experience is a central principle of Reggio-inspired practice. As I began observing more carefully and documenting what the children were up to, I started to wonder: How is the documentation itself a recursive research practice? It seemed the more I documented, the more inquiries I uncovered. I knew that all children are natural-born meaning makers from birth, and I had a fairly well-formed idea of how they inquired into language learning, but I wondered what difference speaking a language other than English makes in the types of inquiries a child pursues and how he pursues them. How could my inquiry into this idea expand the notion of what counts as literacy in my kindergarten classroom?

My own questions led me to pay much closer attention and to carefully document what I saw happening so that I could write about it and share the information with my study group. It was in the company of our group that I realized that everything I was documenting, the "pedagogy of listening" (Rinaldi, 2006, p. 17) I was enacting, was actually valuable data. Carefully documenting our work through photographs, anecdotal notes, observations, and written reflections not only made our work public but also allowed me to more fully develop this pedagogy of listening and to see the centrality of relationships of all sorts in my classroom.

Centrality of Relationships and the Pedagogy of Listening

As discussed in Chapter 2, relationships are central to all learning. In Eric's case especially, his relationships to materials and texts were critical to his literacy learning. As I collected data in my classroom, I wondered in what ways and by what means these relationships were developing. What specific actions and materials support the development of deep relationships from which optimal learning can grow? I first learned about the pedagogy of listening from the educators of Reggio Emilia. The pedagogy of listening is more than physical hearing; it is, as Carlina Rinaldi says, "a metaphor for having the openness and sensitivity to listen and be listened to—listening not just with our ears, but with all our senses (sight, touch, smell, taste, orientation)" (2006, p. 113). This idea made me rethink how and to what I "listened" and to attend to much more than those things I could simply see and hear. Listening in this way forced me to think about the children's theories and questions and opened me up to reconsidering what their ideas and actions really meant. For instance, when Eric chose to sit under the table rather than participate in our morning meeting, instead of determining that he was being defiant or bad, this new sensibility caused me to consider his actions as evidence of something that was not about him but about some relationship, or lack thereof, in the classroom. Putting relationships at the center of my classroom and engaging deeply in a pedagogy of listening gave me and my learners the time and space to negotiate a curriculum that best met all of our varied needs.

Negotiated Curriculum

While I was certainly cognizant of the curricular expectations of my school administrators and of the state academic standards, a curriculum isn't necessarily successful when I decide what to teach, choose one way to deliver instruction, and offer it only at appointed times. Curriculum is whatever happens in a child's day, and the child must be a part of determining that curriculum. My experiences with teacher research caused me to wonder how the dance of negotiated curriculum unfolded. What happens when the child is the protagonist in determining the most appropriate curriculum for himself? My teacher research allowed me to see that Eric was an active protagonist in his own learning, and for lack of any better way to approach him than following his lead, I ended up expanding my notion of what counted as literacy as a result of our year together.

An Expanded View of Literacy

Because Eric initially seemed to be so different from any child with whom I had previously worked, I was forced to step back a little further and then follow his lead to discover what he was actually inquiring about. What I found caused me to reconsider what it means to be literate when you're five or six years old, to question what counts as literacy in an early childhood classroom, and who decides. I was forced to reexamine what I believed about how young children make meaning and represent their learning. What role do texts—both traditional and child-generated—play in developing children's thinking? What is the role of play in learning to read and write? As my understandings grew, I began to wonder how my teacher research could lend credibility to this expanded notion of literacy. I also found myself reexamining the curricular structures of readers and writers workshops in terms of how they support the idea of this kind of meaning making as literacy.

Building Bridges to Understanding

Eric's relationships with materials forced me to expand my notion of what counted as literacy to embrace something greater than knowing all the letters of the alphabet and their sounds or even reading and writing. His continuous resistance to conforming to my conventional academic expectations and his unwillingness to allow me to ignore him finally enabled me to construct images of both the child and the teacher as empowered agents of learning. By practicing the pedagogy of listening, I was able to see the relationships my students were building—not just with me and one another but also with the spaces in our classroom, with the materials I offered and they chose to use, and with the texts we shared—and the critical role those relationships played in helping children make meaning and build connections to school.

In *Creating Classrooms for Authors and Inquirers*, the authors quote Marilyn Greene: "Dewey contended that the self is in continuous formation through action of choice. He also noted that the richness and complexity of selves people create are functions of their commitments to projects they recognize as their own" (Short & Harste, 1996, p. 313). The nature of our work allowed me *and* Eric to finally recognize what we were doing as projects that were uniquely our own, and by collaboratively negotiating our curriculum we were able to choose the actions that we knew would lead to each of us building our identities. Eric's construction of his many buildings is but one iteration of the myriad ways in which children construct their identities and make sense of the world, and his creations remind us that narrowing the opportunities and methods for meaning making narrow the child, and thus our world.

My work with Eric and his classmates changed me as a teacher and as a person forever. Never again will I be able to spend a year with children without engaging in teacher research. Never again will I defer to an "expert" and doubt the validity of my own knowledge when it's been carefully co-constructed with children and other teacher-researchers through extensive research, documentation, and reflection. Never again will I merely listen to children without involving my heart, hands, eyes, and ears—my soul. I now understand much more clearly the monumental task that building meaning is for *all* of us, and I will not allow anyone to narrow a child's opportunities for making sense of this life and becoming a fully literate participant in our democracy.

Making Anecdotal Note-Keeping Easy

I used mailing labels (either standard address size or larger) on a clipboard to keep track of what my kids were up to on a daily basis. I wrote each child's name on a blank label every two or three days. Then I kept my clipboard as a constant companion, always being sure to date my entries. I created a code for the activities in which the children regularly engaged (RW = Readers Workshop, WW = Writers Workshop, MW = Math Workshop, DP = Dramatic Play, etc.).

At the end of most days, I transferred the labels to either a composition notebook I had cut tabs into or a tabbed three-ring binder. This quick technique provided me with a wealth of information about each child's progress and usually spurred me to record further observations, connections, and memories from the day's events. I have experimented with using different colored pens on different days to make the entries stand apart, and when I taught older children, I gave them the labels during workshops and had them take notes about each other.

Bibliography

Cadwell, L. B. (1997). *Bringing Reggio Emilia home: An innovative approach to early childhood education.* New York: Teachers College Press.

Cadwell, L. B. (2003). *Bringing learning to life: The Reggio approach to early childhood education.* New York: Teachers College Press.

Calkins, L. M. (1994). *The art of teaching writing* (new ed.). Portsmouth, NH: Heinemann.

Calkins, L. M. (2001). *The art of teaching reading.* New York: Longman.

Collins, K. (2004). *Growing readers: Units of study in the primary classroom.* Portland, ME: Stenhouse.

Cummins, J. (2000). *Language, power and pedagogy. Bilingual children in the crossfire.* Clevedon, UK: Multilingual Matters.

DaSilva Iddings, A. C. (2005). Linguistic access and participation: English language learners in an English-dominant community of practice. *Bilingual Research Journal, 29*(1), 165–183.

Edwards, C., Gandini, L., & Forman, G. (Eds.). (1993). *The hundred languages of children: The Reggio Emilia approach to early childhood education.* Norwood, NJ: Ablex.

Facella, M. A., Rampino, K. M., & Shea, E. K. (2005). Effective teaching strategies for English language learners. *Bilingual Research Journal, 29*(1), 209–221.

Ferreiro, E., & Teberosky, A. (1982). *Literacy before schooling.* Portsmouth, NH: Heinemann.

Fountas, I. C., & Pinnell, G. S. (1996). *Guided reading: Good first teaching for all children.* Portsmouth, NH: Heinemann.

Freeman, D. E., & Freeman, Y. S. (2004). *Essential linguistics: What you need to know to teach reading, ESL, spelling, phonics, and grammar.* Portsmouth, NH: Heinemann.

Gallas, K. (1997). *"Sometimes I can be anything": Power, gender and identity in a primary classroom.* New York: Teachers College Press.

Gandini, L., Hill, L., Cadwell, L., & Schwall, C. (Eds.). (2005). *In the spirit of the studio: Learning from the* atelier *of Reggio Emilia.* New York: Teachers College Press.

Gómez, L., Freeman, D., & Freeman Y. (2005). Dual language education: A promising 50–50 model. *Bilingual Research Journal, 29*(1), 145–164.

Hubbard, R. S., & Power, B. M. (1999). *Living the questions: A guide for teacher-researchers.* York, ME: Stenhouse.

Katz, L. G., & Chard, S. C. (2000). *Engaging children's minds: The project approach* (2nd ed.). Stamford, CT: Ablex.

Krashen, S. D. (2003). *Explorations in language acquisition and use.* Portsmouth, NH: Heinemann.

Kriete, R. (2002). *The morning meeting book* (2nd ed.). Turners Falls, MA: Northeast Foundation for Children.

McCarrier, A., Pinnell, G. S., & Fountas, I. C. (2000). *Interactive writing: How language and literacy come together, K–2*. Portsmouth, NH: Heinemann.

Moll, L. C., Amanti, C., Neff, D., & Gonzalez, N. (1992). Funds of knowledge for teaching: Using a qualitative approach to connect homes and classrooms. *Theory Into Practice*, *31*(2), 132–141.

North Central Regional Educational Laboratory. (1994). Funds of knowledge: A look at Luis Moll's research into hidden family resources. *CITYSCHOOLS*, *1*(1), 19–21.

Ramirez, J. D., Yuen, S. D., & Ramey, D. R. (1991). *Longitudinal study of structured English immersion strategy, early-exit and late-exit transitional bilingual education programs for language-minority children* (Final report, Vols. 1 and 2). San Mateo, CA: Aguirre International.

Ray, K. W., & Cleveland, L. B. (2004). *About the authors: Writing workshop with our youngest writers*. Portsmouth, NH: Heinemann.

Rinaldi, C. (2006). *In dialogue with Reggio Emilia: Listening, researching and learning*. New York: Routledge.

Rubin, R., & Galvan Carlán, V. (2005). Using writing to understand bilingual children's literacy development. *The Reading Teacher*, *58*(8), 728–739.

Sagor, R. (2005). *The action research guidebook: A four-step process for educators and school teams*. Thousand Oaks, CA: Corwin Press.

Sagor, R. (2000). *Guiding school improvement with action research*. Alexandria, VA: ASCD.

Short, K. G., & Harste, J. C. (with Burke, C.). (1996). *Creating classrooms for authors and inquirers* (2nd ed.). Portsmouth, NH: Heinemann.

Smith, F. (1988). *Joining the literacy club: Further essays into education*. Portsmouth, NH: Heinemann.

Thomas, W. P., & Collier, V. P. (1997). *School effectiveness for language minority students*. Washington, DC: National Clearinghouse for Bilingual Education.

Wong Fillmore, L. (1991). When learning a second language means losing the first. *Early Childhood Research Quarterly*, *6*(3), 323–346.

Children's Literature Cited

Bauers, A. (2000). *Where is Eric?* Crystal Lake, IL: Rigby Education.

Carle, E. (1994). *The very hungry caterpillar*. New York: Philomel Books.

Carle, E. (2004). *Mister Seahorse*. New York: Philomel Books.

Martin, B., Jr. (1983). *Brown bear, brown bear, what do you see?* New York: Holt, Rinehart, and Winston.

Martin, B., Jr. (2003). *Panda bear, panda bear, what do you see?* New York: Henry Holt.

Martin, B., Jr., & Archambault, J. (1989). *Chicka, chicka, boom boom*. New York: Simon and Schuster.

O'Neill, A. (2002). *The recess queen*. New York: Scholastic.

Shannon, D. (1998). *No, David!* New York: Blue Sky Press.

Shannon, D. (1999). *David goes to school*. New York: Blue Sky Press.

Shannon, D. (2002a). *David gets in trouble*. New York: Blue Sky Press.

Shannon, D. (2002b). *Duck on a bike*. New York: Blue Sky Press.

⊚ Research Conversations: Organizing Anecdotal Notes

WITH KAREN K. GOLDSTEIN

JUDY: In this project you use lots of data forms, lots of data sources, but it seems that one of the things you use most is anecdotal notes. Why don't you talk a little bit about how you use them and how you organize them, and then we'll take it from there.

KAREN: I think the basic thing for the notes is that my clipboard each day had every child's name on it. So I had a sticky label with each kid's name on it. And I wrote down whatever was going on, and I developed a code for each activity—RW for readers workshop, WW for writers workshop—and just jotted notes. I tried most days at the end of the day to take a look, and often just simply looking at what I had written would remind me, "Oh yeah, and I saw this too and later this happened."

JUDY: So then did you add notes in later in the day?

KAREN: Yes, usually I did. And I found myself having these new insights, "Oh, *that's* what that was about," and if I hadn't written just the little tiny notes earlier in the day I would never have remembered it at four o'clock.

JUDY: Okay, so your memory is provoked by the short little notes, and then you can actually remember and capture more of the day later after school when it is quieter.

KAREN: Right.

JUDY: So how did you do this physically? Did you transfer the sticky notes to a journal?

KAREN: Usually I would add the notes to my notebook where each person had a tabbed section. And if there was more to say, I could just write as long as I needed to in that tabbed spot.

JUDY: Okay, let me see if I have this right. You have a clipboard with mailing labels for each child set up at the beginning of the day before the children came in, and then you make these little short notes to yourself, because of course you don't have a lot of time. Then later on after the children leave, you would transfer these labels to a binder where each child had a tabbed section. Put the label on a larger piece of paper where you could then use those short notes to provoke your memory and write more.

KAREN: And the benefit for me of having every child's name on there was that I knew who I *didn't* notice at the end of the day. And usually my labels would last for a couple of days for many kids. The ones I was most curious about or frustrated with I wrote more about. But that was a really good sort of control for me.

JUDY: It kind of kept you accountable.

KAREN: Yeah. I would look at the labels and say, "Oh, I haven't even thought about that kid today; I wonder what he's up to—I better make sure I watch him tomorrow, or read with him tomorrow."

JUDY: So just having the labels sort of speaks to you about your own observations because you can see what you have observed and what you haven't observed by what you've written down.

KAREN: And then over time when you collect them in the binder, you can see, "Wow, I almost never take notes on this child; I wonder why that is. Maybe I should pay more attention." They're those fly-under-the-radar kids who do the right things and don't really do anything that stands out or [they] are going along fine. It's good to know when you aren't paying attention to them.

JUDY: So in some ways it actually encourages you to have a democratic classroom with everyone participating equally and hav[ing] equal opportunity. This actually helps you to notice when you're not noticing children in equal ways and to be able to pay attention to them differently.

KAREN: Yes.

JUDY: Tell me more about when you then go back to the binder and look at a section. Say Eric, for example, the boy you focused on in your study. Did you use those notes to find patterns about children? How did you then use those anecdotal notes?

KAREN: With Eric I did. I brought those notes to our teacher research group, and we looked for patterns in both what he was doing and in my responses to him. So there was a real shift in the notes from my being frustrated with him not [being] willing to engage, to a more curious stance on my part rather than a frustrated one. You know, for most of my kids my notes were places I would go back to and ask, "Okay, after two weeks of notes on reading and writing, what's this kid up to?" On a regular basis I don't know that I actually looked for patterns other than what kinds of books they are choosing, what kinds of books they are writing—you know, those kinds of more immediate decision-informing sort of patterns.

JUDY: Obviously, finding patterns can be a more formal research process, and yet finding patterns just in terms of what books children are reading can certainly . . . help with making curricular decisions in a practical way. This reminds me a little bit of the pedagogy of listening from Reggio because they of course are talking about more than just . . .

KAREN: . . . listening with your ears.

JUDY: Right, although the kinds of things you wrote in your notes I'm sure included some listening with your ears. But can you talk a little bit about how this kind of note taking might be related to the pedagogy of listening, and then the ways that this helps build relationships with your children?

KAREN: Well, I think the notes end up being things I've seen, things I've heard, instincts I have, relationships I notice forming. It's so much more than just what you hear with your ears. So I think it allows me to know *myself* better, just by what sorts of things I notice or don't. Because sometimes what's the most telling is, why don't I seem to have any notes on this kid during playtime, or why haven't I ever made any notes about home context with this child?

JUDY: That's really interesting, that the notes actually inform you about yourself.

KAREN: But then that also allows me to build a deeper relationship with a child, because I can go back and say, "Do you remember the other day when we were . . ." And my kids were very aware that I was writing about them. It didn't bother them once they knew what I was doing. I could get out my notebook and say, "Look, I've noticed on this day and this day and this day that you haven't chosen a book, or you haven't chosen this kind of book. What do you think about that? Should we find something different?" I would really involve them and let them know all these notes really say something about them and it's important.

JUDY: How did they react to that?

KAREN: Most of them were very curious when I was sitting there writing. They'd ask, "What are you writing?" I would tell them that I was writing down what they were saying or what they were writing about. But they were always kind of surprised when I'd come back to something and say, "Do you remember when . . .?"

JUDY: Yes, and I bet especially with young children, that they maybe didn't remember?

KAREN: Yes [laughing].

JUDY: To be able to review their own learning through your notes has got to help their learning because they get now an image of themselves as a reader, or an image of themselves as a writer, an image of themselves as inquirers through the patterns that you've noticed, that they might not get otherwise. It's kind of like looking at a photo album. You notice things about yourself, how much you've grown, how much your children have grown. In some ways, I want to say it's such a caring response. Did they feel that? Did they think you cared about them?

KAREN: Oh, I think so, yes. I would often get the question, "Are you going to write about *me*?" You know, if I was talking to this child, "Are you going to write about me too?!" They recognized it as respectful.

JUDY: That you were so interested in them.

KAREN: That whole thing about shining the grow light, from Ruth Shagoury Hubbard and Brenda Miller Power [1999]. That's exactly what that was. I mean, Eric was definitely very interested that I would write about him, especially as his understandings of literacy grew. He could find the *E* and know that's where his label was on my clipboard. For him that was huge. When you pay attention and study something, the children know it's important, and they are more engaged in whatever it is you are observing.

JUDY: You know, it seems we think a lot about materials as part of the environment. But often we think of them only as these concrete things. But they're nearly always symbols of something. And so for Eric, your notes on the clipboard became such a great symbol of his place in the classroom.

KAREN: Yes, that he mattered.

JUDY: He had a physical space where his name appeared a lot and *his teacher* put it there. Your notes became an artifact for him of his relationship with the community and with you that he would not otherwise have. Wouldn't that be a fascinating study, to try to talk to children about how the documentation that we do affects how they think and feel about themselves in the community?

KAREN: When you think about all the practices in the classroom that have no identity of the child attached to it. All those worksheets . . .

JUDY: Or the artifacts that they do have of themselves have become so depersonalized that they're not getting an image of themselves coming back to them. It really comes back to the image of the child again, because now they have a new recourse for building an image of themselves.

KAREN: And Eric *did* that. When you look at the things he did toward the end of the year— When we were using laminating film because we were inspired by Eric Carle's books, he made a piece of laminating film that he put over his cubby name tag. It was a circle with his name on it. I interpreted it as such a statement of "This is me and I can say this." He painted one time all year long, and it was his name and his brother's name and a picture of the two of them.

JUDY: I know there's lots of research about names and their importance to children, especially in early literacy, but I can't help but wonder when he sees you documenting things with his name on it on a regular basis. It's not a surprise that he does that to his own cubby.

KAREN: Right. His name has been elevated to something.

JUDY: Do you have any particular tips or insights for teachers about anecdotal notes?

KAREN: Teachers are worried about writing down the right things or doing it right. And there isn't any "right" about it. Just put something down, even if it's goofy stuff. Just the practice of doing it is valuable, walking around your classroom and jotting things down. It doesn't take time away from your teaching if you're working *with* children and not just dictating to them. You have to be in the moment with the child to actually write about it. The notes become a tool to know the kids and yourself. You can't be the sage on the stage, because that's a performance and not collaboration. You'll be amazed.

JUDY: In some ways, I guess it comes down to relationships again. When we take anecdotal notes, we see the children differently, of course, but also ourselves and our relationships, the way we position ourselves in relation to the children. And of course once we do that, our relationships with the children shift.

4

Navigating Rough Waters with Read-Alouds

Patricia Durbin Horan

It is a beautiful day in late May. I am sitting on my screened-in porch listening to a sparrow busily making a nest at the corner of the house. Her scurrying and diligence bring a smile to my face. While she is toiling away, I am sitting drinking the first cup of coffee of the day, enjoying the peace and tranquility of an hour to myself before my children start to stir. In these few minutes of solitude, I allow my thoughts to wander back over the past school year. The quiet and peace of the morning are as much of a contrast to the year with my kindergarten students as I can imagine. The phrase "What doesn't kill us makes us stronger" comes to mind. I feel the need to write about this year to help crystallize my learning and to bring closure to my experience. As a seasoned teacher, I have had my challenges, surprises, and adventures with children. Usually I find it nearly impossible to think of spending my days in any way other than in the company of children. But this was a year when I cried often and struggled through many days. This was a year when I questioned my career choice.

Background

Over time, I had taught a broad range of students in a variety of settings from second graders to adults. I had run programs for adult learners and tutors, enrichment classes, and remedial programs for at-risk children. I had also learned much from my own four children. Then, through an unusual string of events, I was asked to teach a preschool class in an early childhood program that our youngest child attended. I accepted a short-term, half-day position teaching a special-needs preschool class, though I questioned my suitability as a teacher for such young children. But this early childhood program was inspired by the classrooms of Reggio Emilia, Italy, and I was intrigued by the work being done in this school.

I discovered that I was completely wrong about my fit for teaching in the early childhood field. My experiences with these young children were refreshing, energizing, and completely fulfilling. I went back to my own graduate studies in order to learn about best practices for young children. The following year I secured a position as a kindergarten teacher and prepared for my first year with the enthusiasm and passion of a "new" teacher. I spent hours daydreaming about the delightful atmosphere that would be *my* classroom, one in which dragons would be slain, worms would be investigated, music would be created, books would be relished, stories would be written, and projects of all kinds would be in the works. I cleaned out cupboards and closets. I thoughtfully arranged the different spaces in the room. I visited with my fellow teachers to gather practical ideas.

The look and feel of my classroom was critical to a successful beginning. I embraced the Reggio belief that the environment acts as a third teacher, and this made me reflect about each part of my classroom space in a much different way than I had in the past when arranging my classroom. It needed to be invitational, neat, and organized, with natural light and materials. I was not decorating a room; I was creating a learning environment for children. The space had to be designed to support the specific kinds of instruction I planned to undertake. After weeks of work, everything seemed to be ready for a group of children to have a happy place to live, create, and learn together. The time came for the children to arrive.

Important Literature

In addition to preparing my classroom, I prepared myself by reviewing some of my core beliefs about teaching. I reread the books that had become my "advisers." The books I considered most critical were those about the principles underlying the schools of Reggio, those that supported my teacher research, and those that helped me think about and implement readers and writers workshops. I found myself valuing these three "sets" of ideas because each puts children, and children's work, at the center of the classroom. Each regards children as capable of interesting, important, and inspiring work. None offers a scripted program that suggests one path or one correct response, but instead provides a kind of structure in which children are the leaders of a negotiated curriculum. These teaching ideals rang true for me. This was the way I wanted to teach.

Two principles of the Reggio Emilia approach are most central to my thinking, both of which are discussed more fully in Chapter 1. First is the "image of the child," which positions the child as strong, capable, curious, and full of potential (Cadwell, 2003). I knew that my teaching had to focus on each child's beliefs and strengths. Second, and in a similar way, the Reggio Emilia approach upholds an "image of the teacher" in which the teacher is considered a competent, responsible researcher (Cadwell, 2003). In this role, the teacher-researcher is always observing children in order to uncover their questions and the inquiries they are pursuing. The teacher-researcher also documents learning and creates visual displays of carefully collected and organized artifacts to demonstrate for others the active, creative meaning making of children.

Karen Gallas (1994), the Brookline Teacher Researcher Seminar and Cynthia Ballenger (2004), as well as Ruth Hubbard and Brenda Power (1999) helped me to develop myself as a teacher-researcher by introducing me to a variety of data-collection tools, including field notes and photographs. Vivian Gussin Paley's work (1992, 2000, 2004) influenced me in a different way. Her rich narrative research journals paint an impressive picture of her relationships and work with young children. Reading her work first helped me to see myself in this role of teacher-researcher and imagine myself as a writer of research. I was looking forward to my role as a teacher-researcher in my new kindergarten setting.

Like my colleagues in our study group, I had been studying and was eager to experiment with readers and writers workshops (Calkins, 1994, 2000; Ray, 2004). I especially appreciated the role of reading aloud to children in both writers and readers workshops and was inspired by Mem Fox (2001) and Lester Laminack and Reba Wadsworth (2006) to consider the profound importance of this practice. In fact, read-alouds became the focus of my research.

Classroom Context

I fell in love with each of my students the week before the start of school, during our introductory conferences. Most seemed happy and enthusiastic as I met them one on one with their parents. Some, however, also planted seeds of worry through behaviors and comments. Among my twenty-three children, more than half were or would eventually be identified as having significant medical, emotional, or academic concerns. My initial assessments suggested that most had little exposure to books.

I was determined to maintain my image of the child as capable, curious, and strong, and despite some of the challenging backgrounds of my new students, I was undaunted in my enthusiasm to begin the year as I planned for the kind of beautiful learning experiences I had read about. I set up for readers and writers workshops, planning read-aloud sessions and mini-lessons, large blocks of time for independent work, as well as space and time for community sharing.

I had workshop bags for all the children in which they could keep both self-selected and teacher-selected books. With the help of my instructional assistant, I prepared many little blank books for children to write in and set out large low tables with a variety of appealing writing utensils available.

The first month of school was more than a little challenging. We had temper tantrums. We had crying. At times it seemed we had all-out warfare. The block area was the scene of many of these conflicts. When one child built a structure, other children would take great joy in knocking it down, which led to fighting. Others used the blocks as guns or other weapons. Eventually I closed the block area and later I asked the children to come together in a circle to build a community tower. However, half of the children played with their own blocks and ignored the group activity. Our community tower was knocked down several times in the process.

This atmosphere of violence and disorder seemed to prevail despite all of my attempts to change it. I spent my days putting out fires, soothing children, trying to be in three places at once, and, more often than I had ever imagined, restraining children when they couldn't control their anger. Our classroom was not a happy place. Each day I went home and replayed the struggles of the day, wondering what I had done wrong. Each morning I returned determined to make things better, to begin again. I pleaded for help from my colleagues. I received many words of advice about how to best "control" my class using behavior management strategies for manipulating children to act in the appropriate school manner. But while I tried many of the suggestions, they just did not feel right. I had spent too much time and energy learning and reflecting on best practices with young children. I professed to believe in the Reggio philosophy of education. Nothing in my reading had suggested regimenting and confining children in such rigid ways.

My Study

Luckily, my teacher research group helped me see through the turmoil. Generating constructive inquiry questions helped me sort through my classroom observations and pay more attention to them. When I did, I noticed that when I read to the entire group of children, we had moments of peace. For some reason, by the time the third or fourth page of the read-aloud was turned, every eye was fixed, every body still, and every trouble distant. I wondered what this meant. I wondered if read-aloud texts were helping us in unexpected ways and if I could build on this new knowledge. Finally I decided on the question that would guide my research and my work with the children: *In what ways do my students use read-aloud stories to make connections and build relationships with one another?* Simply asking this question focused my thinking and gave me new resolve. Teacher research was already helping me navigate rough waters.

Research Strategies

I had been collecting children's work and taking photographs since the beginning of the year. I had also begun a research journal but was discouraged by how often I resorted to "venting" rather than recording the learning events of the day and so had abandoned that practice. Now, with a research question firmly and passionately articulated, I went in search of data collection strategies that would help me pursue and answer my question.

Running Records of Classroom Life

Each day I kept a clipboard readily available and often carried it around the classroom with me. I wanted to maintain a more specific record of what was happening in terms of relationships. Because we were using a workshop structure, the children engaged in regular independent reading and writing times that gave them the opportunity to make choices about their reading and writing work. I jotted down notes about things I noticed, such as new friendships being attempted and which activities were being chosen. I wrote notes about children's language use and kept track of questions I wanted to think about later. After school, I took a few minutes to review my notes from the day. These notes were a bit like a running record of the day's happenings.

Record Keeping of Read-Alouds

I also kept track of our read-aloud texts and how the children were using them during independent work times by creating a data grid on which I indicated which books were being chosen and for what purposes. I noted the books children chose to put in their readers workshop bags. I tallied books they chose to help with their writing during writers workshop. I noticed which books one child chose for impromptu reading and noted books that were chosen by multiple children in one setting.

Photo Journaling

Every day I took many photographs of our classroom activities. I stored them on my computer and arranged them in a variety of ways to generate different views of the events of the day. Sometimes I printed individual pictures of significant events on standard paper and then wrote about the picture directly under the photo (see the appendix at the end of the chapter). Other times I arranged the photos in a series to get a sense of the way an event unfolded. Looking back at our activities through photos was the most helpful research tool for me. In the stillness of photographs, I could see peaceful moments and identify places where I could promote relationships and scaffold learning.

Data Organization and Analysis

Like my teacher-researcher colleagues, I accumulated piles and piles of data including daily notes, artifacts of children's work, charts, graphs, children's stories, and hundreds and hundreds of photographs. I organized all the data in chronological order.

For me, analysis began at the moment I selected an event as a source of data—there was some reason that event merited remembering. What about that particular time or event warranted documentation? That was my entry point into making sense of the data. From that point, I sorted the data by how they informed me. Did a piece of data focus on behavior, instruction, learning, individual students, or group dynamics?

I showed some of the data to the children to find out their thoughts and ideas. This was enlightening! They were amazed that I had written down their words and saved pictures of our time together. They began to think of themselves as coresearchers, often stopping me to make sure I was getting their words down or pointing out a photo I should take.

Some data were more useful than others. Setting much of the data aside and honing in on a smaller number of pieces was both a relief and eye-opening. I found that photos were the data source that spoke most forcefully to me. Looking at the pictures and my accompanying comments helped me to follow trends in children's literacy learning as well as their relationships. Stories started to emerge from the data.

Often, data analysis went beyond helping me think about the ways in which the children used read-aloud texts. Data analysis also provoked my thinking and helped me to prepare for the following day and week. Data analysis caused me to think about how I could help lift learning to another level. It allowed me to see children's inquiries more clearly and to think about what materials might be needed to sustain those inquiries. Finally, data analysis caused me to see the questions in my teaching: What books could lead a child or a group of children to a new place as readers? Who was working well together? Who was engaged, who unengaged? Reviewing and carefully considering data was a way to move forward in my teaching.

My study group was always a great resource for helping me to see data in a new way. Sometimes that happened through shared analysis of a specific data source. For example, we developed a coding scheme to identify patterns in my photos. Other times, telling a story and sharing interpretations helped me to blend the data into a meaningful narrative about my own teaching or about my students' use of read-alouds.

Findings

Children's Use of Read-Aloud Books and Shared Language

As I reviewed the different kinds of data I had generated over time, I began to see that each kind of data was informing me in a different way. The chart I had made of our read-aloud texts and how children used them gave me a kind of big-picture answer to my research question. It was clear from these data that children were in fact extending the read-aloud experiences into the rest of the day, both by using the books and by using the language of the books as common ground.

Interestingly, some of the children seemed to be using this common ground of shared language from picture books as a new context for more aggressive kinds of feelings. Books such as *No, David!* by David Shannon and *Beatrice Doesn't Want To* by Laura Numeroff gave the children a kind of permission to assert themselves with the lines "No" and "I don't want to!" The recitation of "Trip, trap, trip trap, who's that trip trapping across my bridge?" in the *Three Billy Goats Gruff* (Carpenter) allowed the students to assume the terrible nature of the troll. The title and line from Sam Lloyd's silly picture book *What Color Is Your Underwear?* provided a context that was less directly personal for the usual childhood talking and teasing about underwear.

Rhyming words and rhythmic lines were also popular with the children. "And it was still hot," the last line of *Where the Wild Things Are* (Sendak); ". . . in a napping house where everyone is sleeping" from *The Napping House* by Audrey Wood; and the silliness of "Silly Sally went to town walking backward upside down!" in *Silly Sally,* also by Wood, have a sense of rhythm that the children seemed to find both fun and comforting. They also enjoyed reciting the entire jump rope rhyme "The Lady with the Alligator Purse," which we had in book form (Westcott).

In fact, rhyme and rhythm were the primary features of the books that the children most often chose at independent learning times. They chose *The Lady with the Alligator Purse* most often, with *Chicka, Chicka, Boom Boom* (Martin & Archambault) a close second. *Silly Sally, The Recess Queen* by Alexis O'Neill, and many other books with rhyme and rhythm were also popular. Children seemed to enjoy the fierceness of the *Where the Wild Things Are* by Maurice Sendak and the troll from *The Three Billy Goats Gruff*, perhaps because the books gave them a safe place from which to express loud, powerful feelings themselves.

Developing Relationships and Community through Shared Meaning Making

My tallying of the children's use of read-aloud books and documentation of their use of book language during the school day gave me some hard data to work with. I was able to see clearly that the time we were spending with read-aloud books was an investment that paid off during the rest of the day. More than that, the students' connections to read-aloud texts and the memorized language moved into their relationships with one another. My photo journaling and use of photo series let me track the ways in which books were bringing children together (see appendix).

In one photo, Jalen, a reluctant reader, is the leader in the rereading of *Chicka, Chicka, Boom Boom* by Bill Martin and John Archambault. I recorded my enthusiasm about this event in my photo journaling, writing the caption "Yeah! Jalen is reading!" under this photo. The girl reading with Jalen is a strong personality, and this makes Jalen's role as storyteller even more impressive. In our study group, we talk about the power of the "big book stand" as a parallel notion to the power of the "author's chair" in writers workshop. In writers workshop, the author's chair is a place where children share their authoring. The big book stand in readers workshop is the same kind of place, where a child can share his or her reading. The person "in charge" of the big book stand seems to be granted a special authority, and as a location of favorite books it wields its own power over the reading activities of the class.

In another photo, I captured Kole and Demetrius sharing close physical space in the round chair. I noted in my photo journaling that they managed this reading of *Brown Bear, Brown Bear, What Do You See?* (Martin) "without controversy." This group of children often did not welcome close physical proximity, yet in this photo the boys are retelling the story as a joint activity, intuitively able to support each other's meaning making. In our study group, we referred to this as "co-reading."

Reading to the entire group had become one of the children's favorite activities. Just about every child wanted to read a book and be in charge of the whole group. But one of my photographs revealed unlikely companions sharing this coveted activity. I still do not know what drew these two together at this moment. They were my most aggressive students. Jacob could seldom sit still for more

The Big Book Stand

Co-reading in the Round Chair

than thirty seconds and had an explosive anger. Amari was rarely interested in listening when we were on the rug together and was my most hesitant reader. I wrote in my journal that day:

> I am savoring this moment that these two chose to read a book together to their peers. A peaceful exchange between these two is a breath of fresh air. It is the first time all day that Jacob has been peaceful.

The fact that both children had a relationship with this book served as a connecting point for the development of a positive relationship.

Finally, one set of photos best illustrated for me the ways in which relationships grow from the common ground of shared text. In six pictures that I took over the span of about fifteen minutes, I could see the progression of one shared reading experience. The first photo revealed Desean and Avionna rereading *The Three Little Pigs* together. These children were two of our class leaders but rarely acted in a positive way toward each other. They did not play together at recess and usually avoided or challenged each other. Here they were sharing the responsibility of telling a story by reading the pictures together. They were hap-

Reading Together Offers a Truce

py, peaceful, and engaged. The next three photos taken during this time span showed others in the class joining in this reading experience. A short time later I took two more photos of the same shared reading.

Developing Relationships through Shared Meaning Making (a)

(b)

(c)

As I reviewed these photos, I noticed Maria for the first time, in the background (photo b, standing at left), and realized that I had not been at all aware of her presence at the time I took the pictures. Only in looking at the series of photos later on did I notice Maria—which caused me to think more deeply about her. I remembered how little Maria had spoken in class. I was reminded that her family spoke only Spanish and that she had not yet connected with the only other English learner in our class, who was a boy. She seemed nearly always to be on the outskirts of our community. As I looked at the photos, I wondered how often I overlooked her because she was quiet and didn't seek attention.

From studying the photos, I saw that after the big book was replaced on its stand, Maria approached it and began to retell the story for herself. I remembered hearing her say the English words with inflection and in characters' voices, a high pitched pig voice and a much lower wolf voice. As I reviewed the photo series, I wondered, "Is she rehearsing the English language? What is she learning about literacy through her retelling? What relationship does she have with this text? How is she connecting to the subject of reading, the earlier group's inquiry?"

Maria Retelling: Building a Relationship with Text

The final photo of the series shows that Aitor—the other English learner—approached Maria during her reading. She allowed him to listen to her version of the book, and I wondered if this was because she knew that he too was trying to find a way to fit into our class. Finally, Maria saw me—and the magic of those moments was gone. But this was a breakthrough experience for Maria and for me. Studying these photos later made me more aware of the "onlookers," those children who tend to stand back and learn from observation. Over time, Maria became bolder in her attempts to participate as she grew in her knowledge of the English language.

Ultimately, photographs were the means by which I made sense of that year in my classroom. Reviewing and writing about photos was instrumental in giving me new awareness of several important relationships that were shaping our literacy curriculum and our life as a community, which I list here and further articulate and summarize in Figure 4.1 (p. 70).

- Relationships between children and the shared language of repetitive text

- Relationships between strong oppositional leaders with a book as common space

Maria Retells for Aitor

- Relationships within a group of peers drawn into a literacy experience though the magnetism of a book and / or their class leaders
- Relationships between onlookers and a group sharing a literacy experience
- Relationships between English learners and read-aloud texts as an avenue into the English language
- Relationships between a group of children who experience social tensions but who find in a book a common place to gather peacefully

What I Take Away from This Study

I do not believe in the idea of "one right answer," and I know there will never be such an answer to my research question. Yet the children taught me so much during the journey of my inquiry. I learned that children develop relationships with peers, texts, and authors through shared experiences within the arena of writers and readers workshops, and that they *can* share space and have close

Data Source	Data	What Relationships?	Interpretation	Curricular Decision	Research Decision
Photograph	• Children in proximity to a book and other children	• Peers • Material	• Children are using books as a mediator. • Children can be in close proximity without conflicts with the common space of a book to share.	• Purposefully allow time for children to explore class read-aloud books during free choice. • Choose read-aloud books that deal with conflict resolution.	• Continue to focus on peaceful moments. • Review photos daily and choose one to write about: "How it helps me know my students."
Read-Aloud Picture Books Data Table (collection of data over a 3-week period)	• Books chosen for individual readers workshop (RW) bags	• Materials • Curriculum	• Children choose books that are familiar. • Children's behavior improves when connected with a book. • The children's relationships with their peers is strengthened through the shared connections with the class read-aloud books.	• Continue to allow for choice in selecting some of the just right books for their RW bags. • Gather multiple copies of these favorite books so more children can have these class favorites in their personal collection of books.	• Continue to keep record of the books children are choosing. • Make note of the impact of having multiple copies of favorite books.

Figure 4.1. Relationality chart for Patty's classroom.

proximity with books as mediators. I have come to see that children can, and often do, naturally scaffold one another's literacy learning when allowed to communicate and have shared literacy experiences to reference. These children taught me that behavior problems can be suspended and improved through the use of shared literacy experiences and that negative student role models can be turned into positive ones through the use of commonly loved texts. Perhaps most important, I have learned that purposeful, repeated use of carefully chosen children's books can create a core of shared experiences and shared language that provides a basis for community.

Epilogue

It is the end of July as I write these reflections. I have had time to soak in the joys and frustrations of this past year. I sit once again on our screened porch, thinking. It is now evening, and after some extremely hot weather in which the temperatures have reached into the upper 90s, a change in the atmosphere signals an approaching storm. The breeze that accompanies the incoming storm is welcome. I silently watch the dark clouds rush closer. The air is thick with moisture as the rain begins. The thunder comes, the lightning follows, and I am reminded of Karen Hankins's (2003) book that I recently finished, *Teaching through the Storm: A Journal of Hope.* She tells of her work with challenging children and describes the storms that she and her class lived through: "My writing served as a much needed calm in the eye of the storm, a breathing space that helped me to find my bearings in the midst of a predictable tempest" (p. 6). I find solace in her words and in the knowledge that my classroom this year was not the first to experience turmoil. I find hope in the fact that writing and photographs helped me in much the same way.

This year of navigating rough waters was the most difficult year of my teaching life. I don't think a day passed without conflict. There was no happily ever after. But, in reflecting on the data and the experience of my study group inquiry, I realize and appreciate with a surprising sense of awe the learning that took place in our classroom. Opening my heart to these children and taking the risk to believe that community was possible for all of us made the difference. I feel honored to have spent this year with them. Parker Palmer puts it this way in *The Courage to Teach*: "The courage to teach is the courage to keep one's heart open in those very moments when the heart is asked to hold more than it is able so *that teacher and students and subject* can be woven into the fabric of community that learning, and living, require" (emphasis added, 1988, p. 11).

To be woven into community—this is what happened in our classroom this past year. The subject of reading, represented to us by wonderful authors in beautiful texts, wove our experiences together in ways the children could handle, and even come to love. With the language of books as our common thread and the bond of shared meaning making, we made something positive of our lives together. I realize that this group, me included, could have easily come undone were it not for the strength I gained from shared inquiry with my study group and the bond the children and I developed through books.

I have always objected to people who seem to have all the answers. As teachers, we are expected to know what will come next and what the path of learning should look like. But the wisdom of teacher research lies in the questions, the thinking, and the reflection. It comes in knowing that every day in the classroom will be a new adventure filled with looking for the inquiries of children, watching for the ways children are pursuing them, and trying to make their learning visible. Teacher research was a lifeline for me at a time when it was intensely needed. It allowed me to watch and learn from the children and to build a community of learners in a class that challenged me in many ways. Through the work of teacher research, I was able to perceive positive interactions between children and to use what I saw to promote further positive experiences. The knowledge that our class could be peaceful and productive within the shared world of a story—knowledge gained only through teacher research—gave us a place to start building unity. Because of all this, I now listen more carefully, talk less often, and notice learning with renewed energy.

Photo Journaling
Photos as a Window into Instruction

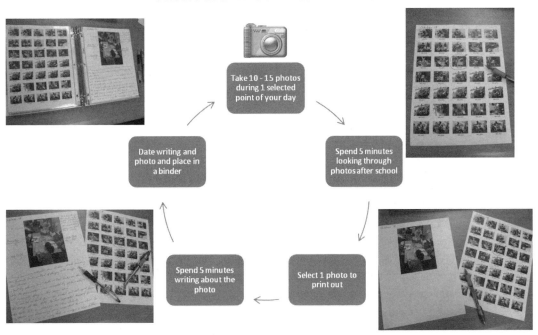

- Take photos each day. At the beginning of the year, take lots of photos throughout the day. After a few weeks, limit yourself—too many photos can be overwhelming.

- Print out thumbnail photos of that day's happenings while the events of the day are still fresh.

- Choose one or two photos to print out that make you think about the instruction or learning. I like to print these as 5" x 7"s so I have room on the page to write my thoughts.

- Spend 5 minutes writing about the photo. Start by looking at it clinically. Who is in the photo? What time of day was it? Where did the photo take place? What was happening in your curriculum? Then write about the learning environment, why you chose that photo, and **most important, how it informs your instruction**.

- Place the thumbnails and the photo with your writing in a plastic sleeve and place it in a binder. This binder will begin to tell the story of your year together. Looking back at this research tool will help you to make decisions about your instruction.

Bibliography

Brookline Teacher Researcher Seminar, & Ballenger, C. (Ed.). (2004). *Regarding children's words: Teacher research on language and literacy.* New York: Teachers College Press.

Cadwell, L. B. (2003). *Bringing learning to life: The Reggio approach to early childhood education.* New York: Teachers College Press.

Calkins, L. M. (1994). *The art of teaching writing* (new ed.). Portsmouth, NH: Heinemann.

Calkins, L. M. (2001). *The art of teaching reading.* New York: Longman.

Curtis, D., & Carter, M. (2003). *Designs for living and learning: Transforming early childhood environments.* St. Paul, MN: Redleaf Press.

Edwards, C., Gandini, L., & Forman, G. (Eds.). (1998). *The hundred languages of children: The Reggio Emilia approach—advanced reflections* (2nd ed.). Greenwich, CT: Ablex.

Fox, M. (2001). *Reading magic: Why reading aloud to our children will change their lives forever.* Orlando, FL: Harcourt.

Gallas, K. (1994). *The languages of learning: How children talk, write, dance, draw, and sing their understanding of the world.* New York: Teachers College Press.

Gandini, L., Hill, L., Cadwell, L., & Schwall, C. (Eds.). (2005). *In the spirit of the studio: Learning from the atelier of Reggio Emilia.* New York: Teachers College Press.

Hankins, K. H. (2003). *Teaching through the storm: A journal of hope.* New York: Teachers College Press.

Hubbard, R. S., & Power, B. M. (1999). *Living the questions: A guide for teacher-researchers.* Portland, ME: Stenhouse.

Laminack, L. L., & Wadsworth, R. M. (2006). *Learning under the influence of language and literature: Making the most of read-alouds across the day.* Portsmouth, NH: Heinemann.

Paley, V. G. (1992). *You can't say you can't play.* Cambridge, MA: Harvard University Press.

Paley, V. G. (2000). *White teacher.* Cambridge, MA: Harvard University Press.

Paley, V. G. (2004). *A child's work: The importance of fantasy play.* Chicago: University of Chicago Press.

Palmer, P. J. (1998). *The courage to teach: Exploring the inner landscape of a teacher's life.* San Francisco: Jossey-Bass.

Ray, K. W. (1999). *Wondrous words: Writers and writing in the elementary classroom.* Urbana, IL: National Council of Teachers of English.

Children's Literature Cited

Carpenter, S. (1998). *The three billy goats Gruff.* New York: HarperCollins.

Lloyd, S. (2004). *What color is your underwear?* New York: Scholastic.

Martin, B., Jr. (1983). *Brown bear, brown bear, what do you see?* New York: Holt, Rinehart, and Winston.

Martin, B., Jr., & Archambault, J. (1989). *Chicka, chicka, boom boom.* New York: Simon and Schuster.

Numeroff, L. (2004). *Beatrice doesn't want to.* Sommerville, MA: Candlewick Press.

O'Neill, A. (2002). *The recess queen.* New York: Scholastic.

Sendak, M. (1988). *Where the wild things are.* New York: Harper Collins.

Shannon, D. (1998). *No, David!* New York: Blue Sky Press.

Westcott, N. B. (1988). *The lady with the alligator purse.* Boston: Little, Brown.

Wood, A. (1984). *The napping house.* New York: Harcourt.

Wood, A. (1994). *Silly Sally.* San Anselmo, CA: Sandpiper Press.

⊚ Research Conversations: Photographs for Reflection

WITH PATTY HORAN

JUDY: Patty, I know that one of the most important ways of generating data for you was the use of still photos. Can you tell me how you used the photos to help you pursue your teacher research question in "Navigating Rough Waters"?

PATTY: At first I would take pictures simply to document how children were using different areas of the room, materials, and who would choose to work together. I would print two or three pictures after school—one photo per 8 1/2" by 11" piece of paper. At the beginning of the research project, I would journal in longhand under individual pictures. This was like taking a second set of observational notes of moments that had passed so quickly during the day. Looking at the photos helped me remember lots of detail about the children's activity and to go back in my own mind and almost be there again with the children. This kind of photo journaling felt right to me. I don't always think of myself as a writer, but I could write from the photos. The writing really helped me to see the activity depicted in the photos in a different way than I had when I first took them. You know, during the day there are so many distractions. It really helps to go back without all the other distractions and without *hearing* the other noises in the room. It helped to focus on what was happening in *that moment,* and it also allows you to observe things that weren't really all that apparent when you took the photo.

JUDY: It seems to me that you are really talking about re-viewing your day.

PATTY: Yes, what is always interesting to me is when I go back and look at photos, I see more of what is happening in the background instead of the main focus of the picture. The focus is what was *on my mind,* what I was looking at. But when I go back and look at the actual photo, it seems I can get a wider view. I can see what's happening *around* the focal children, the things that maybe the other children were seeing, or the things that might have allowed the whole event to happen.

JUDY: You seem to really make use of that stepping back and gathering of other perspectives in your work with the photo series.

PATTY: Yes. Every once in a while you capture an event that really helps you to focus on what's going on. This is my favorite series from the year. The whole thing took place over the span of maybe fifteen minutes. It started with me thinking about my research question and being interested in seeing how the kids revisited our read-aloud texts. These two particular kids were very definitely leaders in the class but oftentimes at odds with each other. They were pretty powerful forces in this kind of difficult class. They got my attention because they were sharing a big book together. To have them doing anything peaceful together was rare. So of course I paid attention and began to take some photos.

When they were reading together, they drew others in because they were leaders, and soon there was a group in this area of the room doing this kind of peaceful reading of a book together. And I thought, that's the end of that. But then later I noticed Maria, who was a quiet English learner and had barely emerging English at that time of the year, in the background of the photos. She had isolated herself with a book in the background. She was an onlooker. She was definitely interested in what was happening with the group and looking at the text, but she didn't join, and then she retreated back to the corner in her chair. Of course, this is just the beginning of what I write about in the chapter. But what is important is that in a year where turmoil was this everyday lifestyle, for this moment to happen gave me an insight into what could bring the children together. . . . I could really see how the text that we'd shared multiple times together as a group could be used as a kind of a peaceful place, a mediating place for children to be calm with one another, to share space with one another.

JUDY: Yes, and the quiet child could also be at home in the community by visiting the books her peers had visited. It sounds like this data, this photo series, allowed you to see possibilities that you weren't really able to see in the midst of coping with this very challenging group.

PATTY: Right!

JUDY: You saw things in the still photos that you couldn't really settle into or make sense of when they were happening because of all the distractions and the emotional turmoil that you yourself were feeling because you were in the midst of it. Not only is "Navigating Rough Waters" a study of how texts mediate some otherwise difficult relationships, but the photos themselves allow you to notice the quiet child because the series itself is quiet. In fact, because they are *still* photos—and not video for example—they invite you to sit quietly yourself and still your usual reactions to the group. There isn't the buzz of the activity, just the still artifact of it. The quiet unnoticed child is suddenly as physically present as the ones who were more vocal because it's a visual form of data. The photos are in some ways serving as an equalizer, putting the quiet girl on equal footing with her more boisterous peers.

PATTY: Absolutely. Obviously she wasn't the focus of my thinking at the time. But the photos pull you back from the emotion, because it's emotional in a classroom full of children. Most of the time it is wonderful emotion, but it can be stressful.

JUDY: You know, we often talk about stepping back from our teaching as a kind of first move in the process of reflection. But it almost feels like there is more going on here for you. Not only are you looking back at a moment and thinking quietly about it, but you consider it with sustained attention and allow yourself to follow multiple explanations. The photos have the effect of stopping time and really encourage this "reentry" into the moment in a deeper way. What was once a passing moment in a very busy kindergarten classroom can now sink into your soul and become part of who you are as a teacher in a way that wasn't possible when it simply occurred in real time.

PATTY: Yes, and the thing about a series of pictures is that you get more than that moment. The series tells a story. You can find a beginning point and follow the shape of the story. The series is for me a kind of narrative. And it is such a different kind of narrative than what you see in a video.

JUDY: It reminds me of the idea of contemplation, which means something like "to consider something with sustained attention." I think of that photo series again. As a viewer, you are invited to consider the intimacy and complexity of the moment because your eyes can rest on the images, take them in, and dwell on their possible meanings. You can do all this because time has been stopped for the moment and all activity has been stilled. Video affords a different kind of narrative.

PATTY: Right. [A photo series] *makes* you think back on things, and you have to define it in your own way, tell the story in your own way, which makes it more a part of who you are.

JUDY: Thanks, Patty.

Thinking across the Curriculum: The Importance of Children's Connections to Peers, Materials, and Home

5

ALYSSA HILDEBRAND

Sasha stands in the front of the community circle with all twenty-one of her peers sitting in our community gathering space in front of her. She begins reading from a small paper book she had written at home.

"I hate you."

"You're ugly."

"You're stupid."

As Sasha reads, a general "Ooooh, she said hate!" arises from the group. Students respond to the story as I thought they might. Sasha reads on.

"Hmmm. . . . How can I make everybody nice? I will think. I guess so."

"Can I play with you, please?"

"Yes, you can."

"Thank you."

"Bye, bye, friends. Good bye!"

Now the students begin to understand the intention of the story. Sasha is trying to bring our community back together again. Her book is a tool for raising questions and thinking about what has been going on in our classroom. The main character in Sasha's story uses mean words. In fact, the phrases "I hate you" and "you're ugly" had been used in our classroom a lot recently. Sasha put our words into her story and then had her character think about how to make "everybody nice." She uses kind words.

Sasha's book became a mediator, a kind of scaffold for her peers. Sasha's story invited other children in the classroom to use the same nice language. She asked them to think about their own language and the ways they had been treating one another. Sasha used the word *think* in her story, a word the children were very familiar with. As a teacher-researcher, I was constantly asking my students what they thought and where their ideas came from. Sasha knew the importance of this word. Her story demonstrates her belief that she can think about things and that she can solve problems. She had power over her actions and through her story some influence on others. This is an example of how a child's

79

writing, a representation of her thinking, became a mini-lesson for the rest of the children in the classroom. The lesson had its own purposes, emanating from Sasha's thinking about the needs of her community.

Sarah's story led me to think about relationships and about the environment as a provocation for children's thinking and the means by which they make connections across the curriculum. Carlina Rinaldi, consultant for Reggio Children and councilor for the municipality of Reggio Emilia, Italy, encourages a social constructivist perspective "where knowledge is seen as constituted in a context through a process of meaning making in continuous encounters with others and the world" (2006, p. 6). Children's relationships, their talk and interactions among themselves and with the materials of their environment, are the vehicles through which connections can be made in the classroom.

As discussed in Chapter 1, one focus of education in the Reggio schools is relationships, a supportive social atmosphere, and the importance of the environment as a "teacher" (Rinaldi, 2006). I have been most inspired by this social constructivist perspective and the ways in which a teacher's image of the child influences how social interaction and exploration of the environment take place. In particular, my experience as a kindergarten teacher made me wonder how these aspects of classroom life help children develop their thinking across the curriculum. I wondered what helps children make these cross-curricular connections, connections necessary for learning and cognitive development generally. The question that guided my teacher research project was: *In what ways do children make connections across the curriculum in a Reggio-inspired environment?*

The Setting

My Classroom Environment

When studying the idea of environment as "teacher," it is easy to get caught up in the beautiful pictures of environments with natural and engaging materials and interesting ways of using light (Curtis & Carter, 2003). However, when I looked more carefully at the thinking and the work of the Reggio educators, I found that they are much more concerned with a larger idea of environment. The talk and the activity, all that constitutes the discourse of the classroom, are critical aspects of the environment and its role as teacher.

I have purposely planned the environment of my classroom to provoke thinking and creativity. The children know they are able to use materials in multiple ways to help them explore ideas. To this end, I encourage my students to be self-directed learners. They understand that it is their responsibility to take charge of their learning. My students and I also work toward a negotiated curriculum. I observe their talk and play to gain information about their interests and make them part of the curricular plan.

Documentation

The importance and use of documentation is also a key component of what I have learned from the educators of Reggio and what I do in my own classroom. As part of my everyday practice, I make notes and take photographs of the children as they are working. Often I compile these notes and photographs on a large piece of sturdy paper and put it up in the classroom. These documentation boards make the children's learning visible to all of us.

Curriculum

Our kindergarten day is loosely structured by patterns of activity rather than a strict schedule. While there are many different aspects of our day, for the purposes of this study I describe those parts of the day on which I focused my data collection.

Project work is inquiry-oriented exploration of child-initiated topics (Edwards, Gandini, & Forman, 1998). Projects usually occur over an extended period of time and may last anywhere from a few weeks to a few months. Most projects in my classroom arise from students' play.

Free play is a time when the room is open for students to choose from a variety of activities such as the writing center, mini-art center, LEGOs, toys, painting, computers, book center, discovery table, science center, and blocks.

Workshop is a structure that supports children's work as readers and writers. I use a writers workshop structure consisting of a mini-lesson, independent/collaborative work, and sharing time (Ray & Cleveland, 2004). When I started readers workshop, I tried to align it with the writers workshop structure I was already familiar with, so readers workshop also comprises a mini-lesson, independent/collaborative work, and sharing time.

The Study

> To learn and re-learn together with the children is our line of work. We proceed in such a way that the children are not shaped by experience, but are instead the ones who give shape to it.
>
> (Malaguzzi qtd. in Edwards, Gandini, & Forman, 1998, p. 86)

I began my study in August when twenty-two full-day kindergartners walked into my classroom. These children represented diverse cultural and socioeconomic backgrounds. Our school community is nestled in a midwestern city, with parents earning their living in ways that placed their families in the working and middle classes.

Data Sources

At first I cast a wide net (Hubbard & Power, 2003) by collecting data on all twenty-two of my students. Data sources consisted of artifacts, photographs, and my research journal. Artifacts included things such as writers workshop books (Ray & Cleveland, 2004), children's drawings, and readers workshop pieces (Cunningham & Shagoury, 2005). My camera was handy and ready to take pictures of students during workshop, project work, and free play. I used these photos to capture examples of children thinking with one another and with materials.

My research journal was an important part of my teacher research work. In it I wrote notes about children, my own thoughts about what was happening, as well as my responses to the professional reading I was doing at the time. In addition to my research journal, I used the printed photos as a journal to reflect on what was happening in the pictures. I kept all photos and artifacts in a binder. For the first several months, I kept anything and everything because I was not sure exactly what would be important to my research question.

In January I decided to take a more purposeful sampling of my students. This allowed me to study the data more closely than I could when collecting data on the entire class. Still, I was interested in getting a broad range of data, so I chose four children who seemed to approach tasks and engage with their environment differently.

Sasha was a quiet child and deep thinker. When she said something, it was profound, and the other children would listen intently to her words. Randy was a social child. He enjoyed building things with his hands and would make literacy connections to his creations. Jeff was a reserved and quiet child who often learned new things by watching others. Mark was outgoing, with a passion for engaging in conversations about his family and about tractors. He tended to think analytically.

After looking at these students' work more closely, I started to see trends in my data. Children were exhibiting three kinds of connections: connections with materials, connections with peers, and connections to home. With these trends in mind, I again began collecting data on the whole group in order to get a sense of whether these trends were representative of everyone—and in fact they were.

What I Found

I illustrate these three trends through vignettes of the children. While the patterns are in some ways distinct, separating children's connections to peers, to materials, and to home fragments the richness of their experiences. Therefore, each vignette highlights more than one of these patterns. For a summary of these connections in terms of my thinking about relationships, see Figure 5.1.

Randy and Jeff: Peer Connections and Connections to Materials

> Collaboration is one of the strongest messages that the environment in its role as the third teacher communicates.
>
> (Fraser & Gestwicki, 2002, p. 113)

My students are immersed in a complex social environment every day in which ideas are transferred from child to child through relationships. The following

Data Source	Data	What Relationships?	Interpretation	Curricular Decision	Research Decision
Research Journal	Children's talk: "Coauthor starts with a *k*."	Peers	Sharing their thinking about writing keeps the writing going.	Have Randy and Jeff share their work at WW share time.	Look through data for more examples of coauthoring. Hypothesize purpose and function of this shared activity.
Research Journal Photographs	Randy and Jeff building candy factory	Materials	Randy and Jeff are using the material of blocks to revisit the idea of the candy factory.	Conference with Randy and Jeff about what they are learning. Possibly encourage new representations of these ideas.	Document conference and building through research journals and photos.
Research Journal Artifacts	Mark's drawings of the photos from home	Materials Home	Creating images of home photos in school provides meaningful bridge to personal experience.	Allow time for all kinds of re-representations (including "copying") of artifacts from children's lives as a means of meaning making.	Collect artifacts. Follow this work to its conclusion.
Artifacts	Mark's book on the "Mustang"	To ideas and the subject of writing	Mark uses writing to invent fantasy work from home experiences.	Conference. Spend more time listening to children read their workshop books.	Record children's stories along with their artifacts. Note generativity of home–school connection.

Figure 5.1. Relationality chart for Alyssa's classroom.

illustrates how children naturally make peer connections while also connecting with materials and developing their thinking. In this example, Randy and Jeff transport ideas and materials from our city project, an investigation into the buildings, work, and attractions of our local area, into writers workshop.

Research Journal: March

During Writer's Workshop, I find Randy and Jeff working together. They are surrounded by paper, crayons, pencils, and a large structure made out of Lincoln Logs. The structure was made by them yesterday. It is a candy factory that includes choppers, conveyor belts, a packaging plant, and delivery trucks. I was very impressed with their elaborate thinking and explanation of the structure.

I wasn't surprised that Randy and Jeff built a candy factory. The class had been interested in candy for a while, and it eventually became a full-fledged project. Students were pretending to sell candy, but we had also made real candy and were in the process of opening a real candy store that would be open to students and staff in the school. As I watched Randy and Jeff, they talked back and forth, pointing at the different parts of the factory. I was amazed at the vocabulary that they were using, and I wondered where they had gotten the idea of a factory. I went over to conference with them. Before I even asked, they started telling me with excitement and enthusiasm what they were working on.

RANDY: We're going to write a book about the chocolate factory. People are going to read it and know how it works!

JEFF: *Coauthor*; it starts with *k*.

RANDY: We need the word *chocolate*. I know it's in the room! [They get up and go over to a sign in the block area, which includes the word *chlt* (chocolate).]

Jeff was writing words on the cover of their book, and I could see that he had already drawn a picture. Drawing was one of Jeff's strongest methods of representing his thinking, while writing came more easily to Randy. These two coauthored books frequently in writers workshop. Many times Randy provided scaffolds for Jeff when they wrote. In this case, Randy gave Jeff an idea about what words to write on the front cover.

Randy led Jeff over to the block area. They found a sign taped to the block candy store that another child in the classroom had made. Randy and Jeff knew they could find print in their environment and use it as a tool to assist them in their writing. Jeff then realized that the word *chocolate* was also written on the dry erase board in the front of the room. So Jeff led Randy over to the dry erase board while I followed with camera and tape recorder in hand.

JEFF: There's one over here and one over there, but we don't know which one is the right one!

RANDY: We could use *chocolate* in the sign language book! I thought it was in there!

JEFF: Let's look at the index!

These boys are making two very evident connections here. Jeff and Randy had established relationships with the materials in the classroom. They knew of three different places where they could find the word *chocolate* in the classroom, and they were comfortable using them as tools. The sign, the board, and a book were materials they used as scaffolds for writing. Jeff and Randy also provided learning scaffolds for each other. Randy helped Jeff organize his thoughts for writing, while Jeff used his emerging literacy skills to find the word *chocolate* in the index.

The boys grabbed the book and headed back to the table. Jeff started drawing pictures while Randy wrote words on a page that Jeff had illustrated.

RANDY: This is the conveyor belt! Then the *t-h-e chocolate* . . . Hey Jeff! Oh yeah, never mind. . . . Or, I can use the book. If you want me to, I will. Hey, I opened the book just to the right page! Then the chocolate, *c-h-o* . . .

JEFF: (referring to his drawing) I made this.

RANDY: Hey, that's good! Why did you make triangles and squares and rectangles?

JEFF: Because remember when they get out of the smusher, they are all shapes, remember? Because . . . they are all red.

RANDY: Oh! Okay, but make some brown!

JEFF: Some of them are red.

Randy and Jeff continued to coauthor and to make connections as they wrote their story. Randy wanted to make sure that Jeff drew the candy using the shapes that were in the candy in the block area candy store. The importance of their relationship is clear in the way they encouraged and complimented each other's work. They also made connections to many different materials in the room, all as they continued to write.

RANDY: Then the chocolate goes into the *kuh, co-con-vay-yah-ar-b-belt*. I wrote one whole sentence on this page. What about the title page and the cover?

JEFF: We can do that after. I need the word *chocolate* for the title page.

RANDY: That's in the book! *Then. T-h-e the-n* . . .

Jeff and Randy talked continuously as they worked. This social atmosphere allowed them to get ideas from each other, negotiate with each other, and provide each other with important supports. Jeff decided to stop writing the words for the cover and start drawing more pictures for the remainder of the book, but Randy tried to keep him on task with the writing, and Jeff eventually decided to go back to working on the cover. The boys negotiated whether to title the book *Charlie and the Chocolate Factory* or *Chocolate Factory*. They compromised on *Charlie's Chocolate Factory*.

Once again these two boys were using peer relationships and their connections to a wide variety of materials to make meaning across the curriculum. They brought ideas and materials from the candy project into writers workshop in ways that inspired their writing. The openness of the physical environment as well as the openness of the curricular structures made these connections possible.

The boys continued their work.

JEFF: Oh, it's raining outside! That means I can't play baseball practice! But I can play with my daddy!

RANDY: [looking over to the window and then spotting some pictures of different block buildings that are arranged by the wall] Hey, Jeff! I remember when . . . I remember when I made this building, it was just me. . . . You weren't here yet!

JEFF: I remember when we built the other one. . . . Me, you, and Allen.

RANDY: I remember when we built this one. . . . Donald made it!

In this vignette, Jeff and Randy generate ideas from their environment in a different way. While looking at the many photos on documentation panels around the room, they reminisce about buildings they created in the past. Here Randy and Jeff demonstrate two different kinds of connections: connections with peers and connections to home. The rain makes Jeff think about what will happen after school; pictures make Randy think about and connect to past block-building experiences.

You may wonder why I included the last excerpt of the students' talk. Some teachers would argue that when children are getting up out of their seats, they are not engaged and not on task. However, I viewed this talk as fuel for writing. One of the purposes of the workshop approach is to allow students the freedom to use talk to make the connections that will become resources for their writing. Jeff and Randy went on to finish their book two days later. They shared the book with the class and, interestingly, explained that their book follows a pattern. Randy tells the class, "Jeff made the picture, then I made the words, then Jeff made the picture, and I made the words." Randy's explanation of the authoring process as a pattern was followed by their reading of the book in a pattern format. First Randy read a page, then Jeff read a page, then Randy read a page, and Jeff read a page. This is an interesting demonstration of peer relationships leading to thinking across the curriculum. For them, coauthoring is a pattern they recognized from our math work.

Randy and Jeff's story stands out in my memory and is included in this study as a prototypical example of my students' fascination with patterning concepts across the disciplines. Connections to peers and to materials fostered this cross-curricular thinking. This vignette also highlights home-to-school connections: Jeff made a home connection from rain to baseball practice to his dad; Randy acquired ideas from home that prompted him to build and write about the chocolate factory.

I learned about another home–school connection a week after Randy and Jeff built the factory and wrote their book. Randy had told his mom about their factory, and she came in to school to see the structure. During her visit, she told me that Randy liked to watch a show on television that explains how things work. Just by looking at the factory and viewing some of my documentation of the talk that surrounded its construction, Randy's mom knew that he must have gotten some of his ideas from the show. The next day Randy confirmed his mother's speculations about the origin of his ideas. These home–school connections are even stronger in the next vignette.

Mark: Connections to Home and Materials

It was early in the morning, and before Mark even took off his backpack and his coat, he ran over to show me what he had brought to school.

"These are my dad's pictures!" he said beaming.

He handed me four photographs, all of which had airplanes in them. Vehicles of all kinds—airplanes, tractors, cars, anything that moved and had a motor—were interesting to Mark.

"There is a Mustang, and they are up in the sky. Me and my dad, we went to an airplane show. It was so cool," he told me as he walked away and put the pictures into his backpack.

Most of the connections Mark made during the school day were to his family. He seemed to use these connections to home to make sense of his world. I thought back to other stories Mark had written recently about his family: his mom breaking her foot; going to a factory with her to see how paper was made. During writers workshop, Mark went over to his backpack, pulled out the photos, and found me where I was conferencing with another student.

"Can I write about these?" Mark asked.

"Of course you can," I told him.

I could see the excitement in his eyes as he found a place in the room to work. Intrigued by the model offered by the photos, Mark immediately began to draw pictures in his book that emulated the figures in the photographs, carefully tracing shapes that looked like airplanes. When he was finished with his story, he came over to me, ready to pour out his story. Mark was an emergent writer. He had pictures and one letter on every page to represent words and to tell his story.

"The Mustang is about ready to pick up off the ground," Mark said.

On this page, he demonstrated his knowledge of planes; he knew there were different types or categories, using an *M* to represent the word *Mustang* in his story. Looking at the second page, he read, "The rocket and the Mustang picked up off the ground. I'm the Mustang and I'm going faster." He included a *P* on this page and pointed to the letter, telling me it was the word *picked*. In this sentence, Mark embedded imaginative language into his story while still telling a story of personal experience that originated with his home life. He was now *in* his story; he *was* the Mustang, the one that went faster.

On the third page, Mark had drawn pictures of two planes side by side, just as in one of the photographs he used as a model. "They're both in the deep blue sky," he read, and a *D* represented the word *deep*. His last page said, "Bye." "The planes are going bye," Mark read. It was a perfect ending for the story.

Here we see Mark using his connections to home to inspire his work in writers workshop. He brought materials from another environment and found space in his classroom environment to explore them, a space in our negotiated workshop curriculum.

Concluding Thoughts: Connections across the Curriculum in a Collaborative Community

Studies have shown that apprentices learn as much from journeymen and more advanced apprentices as they do from master craftsmen. It seems clear, then, that effective learning depends on the availability of peers and their willingness to act as mentors and coaches.

(Wenger & Snyder, 2000, p. 141)

Earlier I introduced you to Sasha. Her story demonstrates the role of children in my classroom as collaborators in constructing curriculum. In this empowered role, Sasha's connections to peers through writing helped the community strengthen its relationships. In the chapter-opening vignette, Sasha shares a story she wrote at home that reflects her thinking about school and her classroom community. She uses the materials and practices of writers workshop to bring a message to her peers. In the second vignette, Randy and Jeff use their connections to materials as well as to each other to think together across curricular subject areas. Their vignette also demonstrates the presence and function of home connections in their negotiation of the workshop curriculum. Mark's story illustrates again the use of home connections to develop thinking in school. Mark also shows us the power of materials from home and how the representation of those materials through drawing helped him connect home to the workshop curriculum. All three of these vignettes showcase peer connections and the shared thinking that went along with them.

It is perhaps not surprising that this study found that peer connections occurred more frequently than other types of connections in the classroom. The children naturally make connections to one another daily. Vygotsky (cited in Pontecorvo, 1993) finds that cognition and shared knowledge are co-constructed in interactive settings and that social interaction is an essential variable of development and learning. Our classroom community was clearly founded on relationships within which talk and the collaborative use of materials supported everyone's learning.

In this study, I sought to discover the ways in which children think across the curriculum in an environment that relies on relationships and shared activity to support thinking. Sasha, Randy, Jeff, and Mark provide us with examples of children's relationships with one another, with materials, and with home that develop by thinking together within shared activity. I believe that it is vital for teachers to ground their teaching in shared activity in order to encourage children to think together and across the curriculum. Teachers can establish a classroom environment in ways that support shared activity, activity that facilitates the free exploration and establishment of relationships with peers and with materials. In addition, the environment should be one that invites children's powerful connections to home into the classroom through a negotiated curriculum. When children have opportunities to connect in personally meaningful ways with one another, with materials, and with their home experiences, they develop a rich network of shared thinking. All of this is dependent on a teacher's image of the child. When the teacher sees children as capable and trusts them to co-construct curriculum, when the teacher encourages children to share their thinking, to speak and listen to one another, to work and play together with many and varied materials, a potent kind of learning occurs.

Bibliography

Cadwell, L. B. (2003). *Bringing learning to life: The Reggio approach to early childhood education*. New York: Teachers College Press.

Cunningham, A., & Shagoury, R. (2005). *Starting with comprehension: Reading strategies for the youngest learners*. Portland, ME: Stenhouse.

Curtis, D., & Carter, M. (2003). *Designs for living and learning: Transforming early childhood environments*. St. Paul, MN: Redleaf Press.

Edwards, C., Gandini, L., & Forman, G. (Eds.). (1998). *The hundred languages of children: The Reggio Emilia approach—advanced reflections* (2nd ed.). Greenwich, CT: Ablex.

Fraser, S., & Gestwicki, C. (2002). *Authentic childhood: Exploring Reggio Emilia in the classroom*. Albany, NY: Delmar.

Hubbard, R. S., & Power, B. M. (2003). *The art of classroom inquiry: A handbook for teacher-researchers* (rev. ed.). Portsmouth, NH: Heinemann.

Nicolopoulou, A., & Cole, M. (1993). Generation and transmission of shared knowledge in the culture of collaborative learning: The fifth dimension, its play-world, and its institutional contexts. In E. A. Forman, N. Minick, & C. A. Stone (Eds.). *Contexts for learning: Sociocultural dynamics in children's development* (pp. 283–314). New York: Oxford University Press.

Pontecorvo, C. (1993). Forms of discourse and shared thinking. *Cognition and Instruction, 11*(3–4), 189–196.

Ray, K. W., & Cleveland, L. B. (2004). *About the authors: Writing workshop with our youngest writers*. Portsmouth, NH: Heinemann.

Rinaldi, C. (2006). *In dialogue with Reggio Emilia: Listening, researching and learning*. New York: Routledge.

Wenger, E. C., & Snyder, W. M. (2000, January-February). Communities of practice: The organizational frontier. *Harvard Business Review, 78*(1), 139–145.

◎ Research Conversations: Analyzing and Reflecting on Data

WITH ALYSSA HILDEBRAND

JUDY: What was the most important data strategy that you used as a teacher-researcher?

ALYSSA: I think that keeping the children's artifacts and my own journal writing were most useful to me. Collecting all things children created and then looking for trends in the data, you know those reoccurring patterns. And then using professional readings to back up and understand what I was seeing. It was a blast. That was really fun.

JUDY: I wonder if you can describe your data analysis for me. How did you arrange your data?

ALYSSA: At the beginning of the year, I had a binder and I had each kid's name on a tab. I knew that I was looking for the connections kids were making across the curriculum in a Reggio-inspired environment, but I didn't quite know the direction that would take. So I began gathering things like writers workshop books and other things that represented these connections and other important experiences.

JUDY: So you collected things and organized them according to who created them so you could begin to get a picture of what individual children were doing.

ALYSSA: Yeah. So the first kid that really stuck out to me was Randy, because he was building all these things with blocks and making these great connections. He started to make different representations of a monument downtown. He made them with blocks and then with clay. He made it with little wooden pieces, magnets, all sort of things. So I started really thinking about children's relationships with materials—but back to the data collection. Any time that a child got a connection from Randy, I would put that piece into his part of the binder.

JUDY: So you physically made the connection in your data binder that you had seen in the classroom.

ALYSSA: Right. And then I would try to journal at least two or three times a week.

JUDY: You were a faithful writer during this project. You gathered ideas in bits of text from outside experts and then wrote about them. You did a lot of thinking on paper by putting your voice alongside theirs.

ALYSSA: Yes, and I had all this information! After a while I had to narrow it down to a few kids because I couldn't keep up with all the data and keep writing.

JUDY: Okay, so let me back up a little bit. At the beginning of the data collection, you had your binder tabbed by individual children. Then when you started to see patterns, for example, this child starting to make connections to materials, you had the photographs of him making those connections and the artifacts that he created and put them in the binder with his tab.

ALYSSA: Along with my journal notes.

JUDY: So even during data collection, you were really making analytic moves. When you say, "Okay, there are these patterns emerging so I'll organize this way," you're doing analysis. So later on in the study when you had child-to-child, child-to-materials, and home–school connections as emerging categories, did you then make sections for these?

ALYSSA: Once I made distinct categories, then I rearranged the binder by those categories. And you know, a lot of the ways that I also found those trends was through my journal writing. I would go through and I would reread my notes, and I would take different color markers and start highlighting my field notes and my response writing to professional readings in light of those connections. I might use a blue marker for child-to child connections, and anytime I saw that, I would highlight [in] blue. I had to have a substantial amount of writing before I could do that, but I went back and did blue for any social connection [and] orange for any home connection. And I used that highlighting as a coding method.

JUDY: I see.

ALYSSA: Two of the kids I write about, Jeff and Randy, weren't children I focused on initially, but I ended up focusing on them because all three connections were so strong with them: child-to-child, child-to-materials, and home–school.

JUDY: So it wasn't just children making connections but the strength of the connections within your classroom as well.

ALYSSA: Yes, and it took me looking at everything to find these patterns across the whole group, and then choose a few children.

JUDY: So finding the pattern kind of gave you the lens to be able to notice, "Oh, I've got to get that," even though it was outside of the children that you had originally focused on. Finding the patterns gave you a kind of lens that let you see the importance of what the other children were doing.

ALYSSA: Right, right.

JUDY: Well, it's been really interesting getting a sense of your approach to analysis. Your work really demonstrates the recursive aspects of teacher research, the back and forth of it all, and also of course how your organization of data helped in that analysis. Thanks a lot, Alyssa.

6

The Power of Relationships

JENNIFER WHEAT

The idea of teachers "doing" research and the power behind this research are not new concepts. Lytle and Cochran-Smith (1992), Kincheloe (2003), and Bissex (1994) have discussed the importance of teachers conducting research in their classrooms in order for change to occur. Though this idea may have history on paper, it became reality for me only during my fourth year of teaching, when the printed words on the page became a lived experience for me and for my classroom.

That year, my colleague and friend Judy Lysaker introduced me to teacher research. At first, I was timid about the idea and unsure about the big task of "research." I wondered if I was capable. But with some guidance and nudging, I soon began to realize that research was already a part of my life as a classroom teacher. Like most teachers, I was constantly observing, taking notes, analyzing, interpreting, and making decisions about children and their interactions. It was now time to be more intentional about this practice. I began a year of purposeful teacher research, a year that would profoundly change my view of children and my outlook on teaching and learning.

As I entered my kindergarten/grade 1 classroom that fall, I had already developed a set of beliefs about children and about teaching. Like my study group colleagues, I had been inspired by the work of the municipal early childhood schools in Reggio Emilia, Italy, and grounded my practice in many of the Reggio fundamentals (Cadwell, 1997) described in Chapter 1. I saw the child as a protagonist in his or her own learning, one who is "strong, rich, and capable" (p. 4). I believed in the idea of the environment as a teacher (Gandini, 1993) and prepared my classroom environment accordingly. I understood the use of projects and documentation within projects. Finally, I believed in learning to read and write through a readers and writers workshop approach (Calkins, 2001; Ray & Cleveland, 2004; Collins, 2004; Fletcher & Portalupi, 2001).

I also embraced the idea that teachers act as facilitators who guide children in their learning and that the teacher's relationships with children, as well as children's relationships with peers, adults, and the curriculum, are important to that learning. As I thought about these relationships, I was reminded of Skolnick's (2000) ideas about relationships and literacy. She discusses this in depth and uses Sarason's (1982) framework, including teacher–child, child–child, teacher–curriculum, and child–curriculum relationships. As I looked at all the various relationships within the classroom, it became evident that this was something worth studying more deeply.

In this chapter, I tell the story of a year of research that was guided by a question that evolved over time: *In what ways does observing and writing about children's learning lead me to a deeper understanding of the relational textures in which the learning is embedded?* Through the presentation of data, I demonstrate how teacher research changed my classroom and opened my eyes to a new awareness of the importance of relationships in the classroom. In particular, I highlight the story of one child and his relationship with the classroom community. Finally, I explain the implications of these relationships to our curriculum.

Classroom Context

Take a walk with me through our classroom. The room is silent before the children arrive, but it is not empty. Pictures of each child's family welcome everyone near the entryway. The walls of the classroom are covered with documentation of children's work: charts display their thinking, artwork shows their creativity, and pictures of them busily working inspire further thinking, reflection, and reconsideration.

This documentation was an important aspect of our classroom life. I took photographs of the children at work daily and used the photos to display their work, along with their own commentary written alongside. Often I took time to listen to the children's words and write their comments next to my photos, but at other times I gave the children the pictures so that they could do it themselves—write what was happening during their work. The children and I created documentation panels from these pictures and narratives that told the story of things we were studying.

I placed tables throughout the room strategically, carefully thinking about the advantages of high and low tables, the space between tables, the acoustics of the room, etc. (Taberski, 2000). Some tables seated six, others just two. Some had chairs; others invited children to sit on the floor. The children were able to choose spaces for themselves that would be comfortable for their learning and enable them to work collaboratively with those around them. The organization encouraged fluidity of movement throughout the room, so students could interact with a variety of peers at a variety of times. This space fostered relationships that were dynamic, that could change and grow over time (Skolnick, 2000; Gandini, 1993). This broader sense of space, one that acknowledges both its physical and relational qualities, qualities that encourage encounters with others and with the materials that surround them, was especially important to me that year (Cadwell, 2002; Fu, Stremmel, & Hill, 2002; Edwards, Gandini, & Forman, 1993).

Curriculum

The set of beliefs I adopted as my own from Reggio influenced my curricular decision making. I encouraged the children to take ownership of their surroundings and their learning, as well as to take risks and build relationships that would support them. To make relationship-building possible, I gave the students many opportunities to make choices throughout the day, a process supported through open-ended curricular structures. The main structures of my classroom consisted of readers workshop (Calkins, 2001; Collins, 2004), writers workshop (Ray & Cleveland, 2004; Calkins, 2001; Fletcher & Portalupi, 2001), math workshop, and the project approach (Katz & Chard, 2000). All of these structures helped children become independent learners and problem solvers.

An important quality of these structures is predictability. Calkins (1994) suggests that readers workshop should be a simple, predictable structure because the children's work will be "changing and complex" (p. 32). When I adopted this idea, I put structures in place that were predictable yet flexible: workshops and project time usually took place at the same time every day, but if we needed to change the order of things, we did. Other aspects of our day included interactive writing, shared writing, poetry reading, word work, etc. Together these elements created a comprehensive literacy environment.

Although I had been inspired by many Reggio fundamentals over the years, I did not completely understand them until I began another journey in my career. That journey—teacher research—led me to open up the classroom even more and give children even greater opportunities to be themselves and show their strengths. In fact, teacher research was a part of the Reggio approach that I had been ignoring. In the Reggio preschools, teachers revere children's work and study it deeply to see what children can do. They marvel over its beauty and use all of its strengths to guide them in their next steps. The practices of observing closely, listening intently, documenting work (data collection), reflecting on it, and then beginning the cycle again represented new understandings for me.

Hubbard and Power (1999) suggest that this cycle is natural to teachers, though embedding this work more systematically deepens the everyday practice. Teacher research allows us to analyze the classroom through a different lens to better understand the occurrences in the classroom. Once teacher research was introduced to me, my image of the child changed because I became much more aware of children—of what they can do and just how much I can learn from each of them.

Although I'm describing change that occurred in my classroom, it did not happen in solitude. In Reggio, teachers gather together to reflect collaboratively on their documentation of classroom activities and interactions. Similarly, I had a study group that supported me along my journey into teacher research. Together, we formed a community of practice (Wenger, 1998) that became a place where our writing was surrounded by talk, data analysis, and meaning making. Teacher research became a way of life. Not only did I have outside support, but also I was fortunate enough to have additional colleagues in the classroom: Judy; Emily, a student from a local university who was also learning about teacher research; and an instructional assistant. As we discussed the art of teaching on a weekly basis, I began to understand the act of ongoing collaborative research that I had studied but, until then, not lived myself.

The Study

Data

I chose observation as my primary mode of learning about my students during this year of research. Through these observations, I tried to experience classroom life from their perspective (Corsaro, 1985). This emic perspective required that I not make assumptions about children from the things I could see on the outside, but instead step inside their learning and see them from the inside. I took anecdotal notes (Owocki & Goodman, 2002) and field notes (Hubbard & Power, 1999) as I observed the children, which later became points of reflection. I also took photographs, conducted informal interviews, and analyzed students' written products.

Writing had a new and powerful role as a part of my research. I found that regular writing allowed me to study the actions of the children more closely and to develop interpretations. I took time to write brief notes throughout the day. Then, on Saturday mornings, I headed to my favorite writing spot to think about a particular literacy event that had occurred that week and create what Hubbard and Power (1999) describe as "cooked" notes. I wrote out the entire story of the event. Each time I did this, I was able to examine the situation more closely and come to new understandings that would allow me to be more responsive during my upcoming week with the children. Writing became a way of knowing (see the appendix at the end of the chapter).

All of this allowed me to redefine my role as teacher-researcher. My goal was to discover more deeply the nuances of children's learning and the beautiful texture of the relationships in which that learning was embedded.

My Participants

Our community of learners consisted of eighteen vibrant five-, six-, and seven-year-olds. One of the beauties of the multi-age classroom is that it allows me to develop deep relationships with children and know them well because I have students for two years in a row (both kindergarten and first grade). Each year, only half of my class is new. This lets me begin observing the kindergartners as they enter school while extending the relationships I have with the children and families I worked with the previous year. I make home visits two years in a row, invite families to trimester events, and attend other occasions involving children and their families. This helps me to build deep relationships with my students.

Though my research informed my teaching and learning with *all* of these children, when reviewing the data I was collecting, I became fascinated with one particular child, Thomas. I was especially interested in the ways in which he developed over time and the impact that various relationships had on his development.

At the time of the study, Thomas, a six-year-old African American boy, entered the classroom in sadness. His father had passed away when he was three years old. Pain seemed to accompany Thomas to school every day. He often entered the room solemnly and would distance himself from the group. Hiding under tables, tearing up paper, crying, and other expressions of distress were not uncommon for Thomas.

Thomas's story occurred over his kindergarten year, and though the pages here seem inadequate, my hope is that they will give you a glimpse of this young child, how he evolved over time and the power of relationships in his development as a beginning student. Because writing was my primary method of making meaning and of generating and analyzing data, I have chosen to use excerpts from my writer's notebook to tell Thomas's story.

The Story of Thomas

Meeting Thomas for the First Time

On August 1, Thomas entered the room for our ice cream social—a night for students to visit the school and meet the teacher and other children, become familiar with their classroom, and of course eat ice cream. I walked over to greet him as he hid safely behind his mom. With some coaxing, I was finally able to talk Thomas into posing for a picture . . . no smile though. But as I peered into his eyes, I hoped I would get to know this child well, and I set a goal to build a relationship with him that would help him move beyond the shyness I observed at this first meeting.

I began writing about Thomas early in the semester. On August 10 I wrote about his limited interactions with those around him, as well as with curricular tasks. My first day of writing was full of questions. I knew if I was going to help Thomas be successful, I had to find out what it was about the environment, my teaching, and those surrounding him that acted as barriers to involvement, and most important, what would help him break through those barriers. My image of the child helped me realize that Thomas was capable; it was up to me to study the environment and the relationships, both fundamentals of Reggio, to determine how to help him be successful. I recorded my first wonderings about Thomas's relationships, asking such questions as:

> Writer's Notebook Entry 8/10
> Is it [the task at hand] too overwhelming?
> Does he need to build confidence in his abilities? How am I going to help him build this confidence?
> Why was he making these noises? I need to watch for this to see if it reoccurs and if so when?
> Why the change? Is it because he feels successful? If so, what are ways to make him feel successful in other areas?
> Why the difference from morning to afternoon?
> Does it just take that long to get acclimated to the environment?

As I wrote, I came to realize that Thomas had experienced some successful moments during the day and that it was my responsibility to begin figuring out why some moments were successful and others were not. To help him engage more fully in the classroom, I knew that I needed to think about the instructional, environmental, and relational decisions I had made (Lysaker, 2004). If I did this, and made adjustments, I knew Thomas would be capable of participating more fully in the community.

I noticed that Thomas's relationship with materials seemed to help him feel successful; he was always able to locate, choose, and use the things he needed. This led me to consider that the barrier to engagement might be the actual task, which means that I needed to think of ways to scaffold the task. I also noticed that his interactions with others were very limited throughout the day. In fact, most of his interactions were with me as I guided him in learning. With seventeen other students in the classroom, Thomas's solitude was noticeable. Though it seemed that he spent most of the day struggling with something inside of him, he did have moments when he was smiling and happy. This became my focus: to notice, celebrate, and foster these moments of success.

Beginning the Work

Knowing that I needed to watch for moments in which Thomas was successful and to carefully consider *why* they were successful, I continuously observed and wrote notes about his interactions. Later in the fall, I began to see how these notes helped me make instructional decisions.

Soon thereafter Thomas participated in the entire forty-five minutes of readers workshop for the first time. I sat and wrote about it. This writing allowed me to break down the time that he spent with his partner during that workshop and to see more vividly why Thomas experienced success. That success seemed very much connected to his relationship with a friend, Bradley.

> Writer's Notebook Entry 9/29
> The children's partners changed today. When Bradley was announced as Thomas's partner, Bradley's smile gleamed on his face as he cheered. I smiled, elated that Bradley wanted to be Thomas's partner, and took a deep breath as I looked at Thomas's reaction. His too was a smile. This pair was put together strategically, remembering back to the day that Thomas chose Bradley to be his partner for a penny dice game. At that time I realized that the boys had a connection—not an explainable one because they have two very different personalities, they're at two very different levels developmentally and academically, and their ages are almost 2 years apart—a connection that can only be defined by observation of interactions between the two and their discourse.

Later in the same entry I wrote:

They went to their next literacy station: "Act it Out." Here, Bradley read *Panda Bear, Panda Bear* as Thomas pretended to be each animal in the story. Bradley was practicing fluency and expression as Thomas was making meaning of the book through motions and developing an understanding of how that works, not to mention that both were building a foundation for their friendship.

My intentional—relational—decision to pair Bradley and Thomas was made based on prior observations of the two becoming friends and working together. Bradley was able to accept Thomas's difficult moods, learn from him, and encourage him in their activities. Thomas was able to show Bradley proper procedures and share what he could do. One aspect of his success that day stemmed from this friendship, but it did not stop there. This scenario also illustrates the ways in which Thomas had success with materials, the curriculum, time, and his environment. Having the choice of when to change literacy stations and the freedom to choose materials allowed the boys to find a spot where both could experience success while at the same time challenge their own thinking.

Though Thomas had success on that day in September, he still experienced many days of strife. I continued to observe and analyze these occurrences to determine what would best help him get through the day and what kinds of things seemed to hinder him.

Things Begin to Change

One shivering winter morning, Thomas's experience of writers workshop changed: he chose to write an entire book for the first time. Over the weekend, I looked closely at the photographs I took during that workshop, listened to the audio recording, and then wrote about the experience.

> Writer's Notebook Entry 1/18
> Thomas rushes to the collection of blank books and decides to choose a book where he can draw pictures and write words. He notices his friend Rosie, and sits down next to her. She sees the book he's chosen, quietly gets up, and walks over to pick up one just like it. On her way back she strategically selects a grey marker (Thomas' favorite color) and sits back down next to him.

Again, the children's relationships with materials are important. They know where materials are and how to use them. This knowledge allows them to choose the materials that will work best for them. Had I given Thomas the book he picked on January 18 at the beginning of the school year, he would likely have shut down, his typical reaction when presented with something he found overwhelming or too hard. The distance between the curricular task and his readiness for that task would have been too great. But here in January he was able to choose this book and also use those around him to be successful. Now he was ready for it, whereas he had not been earlier. Giving the children access to a variety of materials enabled them to take up the challenges for which they were ready. Additionally, it was obvious that Rosie and Thomas had a special friendship and that she understood him. She knew he liked the color grey. She knew that he liked *The Three Little Pigs*. I could see that Rosie and Thomas's relationship enhanced his relationship with the curriculum. Rosie knew how to reach out to Thomas with his favorite book and his favorite color, allowing him to become successful during this writers workshop. It gave him a way to connect with and become a full participant in the curriculum instead of acting as a bystander to learning. This one small scenario underscores the importance of a relationship between materials, friendship, and the curriculum.

In this excerpt from that same notebook entry, I focus on how the use of space shaped peer relationships. It is notable that the two children are able to work closely together and choose where they want to sit.

> Writer's Notebook Entry 1/18 (continued)
> Their chairs are close to one another, so close that they sometimes touch elbows, shoulders, or their arms cross. Her gaze fixated on the paper as Thomas is nearly shoulder to shoulder with her, his eyes peering at her hand drawing the wolf as if he's studying what she's doing. They continue to work together closely, eyes and hands busy. As they continue to cross space, Thomas points to his picture as she turns the page of the book.

My decision to let the students choose their own seating throughout workshop time was a relational, environmental, and instructional decision that enabled Thomas to be successful during this activity. It was relational and environmental in the sense that students chose the peers they would sit with and where they would sit. In this instance, Thomas and Rosie sat together for about forty-five productive minutes. The decision was also instructional because it was based on my image of the child. Since I viewed each child as strong and capable, I trusted them to use one another to grow and learn. The payoff can be seen in Thomas's close proximity to his friend, who helped him create his book and allowed him to sustain his writing.

This was also the first time that Thomas reached out to share what he is doing with his family at home, moving beyond our classroom community.

Writer's Notebook Entry 1/18 (continued)
When Thomas finishes, he is ecstatic and wants approval to take it home. I ask if
we can copy it first. He says "yes" and we walk down to copy his important work,
his book, his writing.

Thomas was so excited to show his mom and brothers the work he had complet-
ed. Through this and many other moments, I continued to learn from Thomas
and to think about how to design curriculum that invited him in and helped
him succeed.

Writing about this illuminating literacy event allowed me to relive the experience. As I read through this excerpt from my notebook, I was thrilled that
Thomas was a willing learner because he had found a way to relate to what
we were doing, and because his friend Rosie helped him with that. Here, their
friendship and understanding of one another supported success.

I was not the only one in the classroom who began to understand how
important relationships of all kinds were to Thomas. The rest of the classroom
community also realized this, especially the girls. The bond that many of the
children had made through their friendships with Thomas became clear in mid-
February. Thomas had not been in school for a week, and several of the girls
were sad about his absence. One Friday morning they came in, wishing Thomas
would be back. Their wish came true. Thomas was at the door, and I knew that
after being absent an entire week, he would need some time to adjust. I quickly
greeted him.

Writer's Notebook Entry 2/11
I head towards [Thomas] in the hallway to give him a hug. "Wow. You've gotten
taller—at least 5 inches," I joke. He laughs and says yeah and then puts his head
down. I leave him in the community to give him space.

But, as so often in the past, I learned through observation that space might not
be all he needed. He needed to know that everyone cared about him, and the
girls in the classroom showed him just that.

Writer's Notebook Entry 2/11 (continued)
He now was outside the door looking somewhat sad as though he was already
deciding how his day would be. Then I hear a few friends say, "Thomas is back!"
Next thing I noticed, Rosie walked over to him before even coming into the room
to give him a picture she had made. On the back, written in his favorite color grey,
was "to Thomas, from Rosie." Bethany then joins them. As they walk in the class-

room, shoulder-to-shoulder, both girls begin chanting: "Thomas is back, Thomas is back."

The girls expressed their excitement about Thomas's return verbally, and Rosie did so also through writing, creating a card for him using his favorite color. Rosie not only expressed the importance of their friendship, but she did so once again through the use of materials, the grey marker.

Natalie then joined Rosie in the gift giving.

Writer's Notebook Entry 2/11 (continued)
Natalie then pulls out a paper from her bag. She walks over to [Thomas] and gives him the picture. She too had his name and her name on the paper with grey marker. It's amazing that these two little girls were thinking of Thomas in a different setting—Loving Care: an after school program that he does not go to. They truly missed him and have such a heart that they wanted to do something to make him feel welcome, to make him feel good.

The girls came into the classroom with a picture already "addressed" to Thomas, which showed that they were thinking of him beyond the classroom community, thus demonstrating how classroom interactions reach beyond the four walls of school into other areas of the children's lives. I am reminded of Cadwell's (2003) reference to hearing Carlina Rinaldi's (1992) thoughts on relationships: "The best environment for children is one in which you can find the highest possible quantity and quality of relationships" (qtd. in Cadwell, 2003, p. 106). When these classroom relationships are strong, they begin to seep into other areas of the children's lives and then other aspects of our lives connect to the classroom. Gandini (1993) discuss the importance of the home–school connection, or community-school connections. This nexus of relationships demonstrates that the school and the greater community are connected in various ways, and we must allow these community connections to be part of classroom life.

The girls continued to draw Thomas into the community that morning, and they seemed to purposefully help him reacclimate to the environment.

Writer's Notebook Entry 2/11 (continued)
Rosie went over and gets his reading folder and brings it to him. Erin joins them. Thomas chooses to stand at a table. The girls ask if he wants a chair. He does not. He wants to stand. The girls situate themselves around the table and close to Thomas. They begin to read. Rosie pulls out the stickers she brought that were like his. She begins to give him some. Technically, that's not what they should be

doing but I knew that's what he needed. He needed to see ALL the ways his community supported him so I watched as she gave him stickers.

This particular moment highlights the importance of Thomas's friends and the materials that engaged Thomas in the morning activity of reading. The girls took on an almost motherly role, making sure that he was comfortable and being available to him if he needed help. Rosie's special friendship with Thomas is highlighted again when she shares the stickers with him. My role as a teacher-researcher allowed me to pause and just observe. Even though the stickers were off limits at this time of the day, I could see that they were a way for Rosie to connect with Thomas. Being a researcher as well as a teacher gave me time to think, time to remember that "getting what you need" is fair. Thomas was getting what he needed. Through the research and writing process, I realized the need to slow down and think about something before responding.

The girls continued to assist Thomas in their own way. Natalie, one of the older children in the multi-age classroom, knew that it was a time to read, and she took it upon herself to help Thomas.

> Writer's Notebook Entry 2/11 (continued)
> Natalie pulls out the *Chicken Soup with Rice* book, one of his favorites, and begins to read and have him say some of it too. He wasn't as interested as she would have liked him to be because he was busy with his stickers. So she pulls out the *Red White and Blue* book, another one of his favorites, and they read together. Finally, the ABC Pop book is brought out and they converse about his favorite part, the hot dog page.

Here, Natalie uses her knowledge of Thomas's relationship to the curriculum (in this case, books as materials) to engage him in reading. She knows the books he likes and even his favorite parts well enough to know what topics to bring up for discussion. In this example, Thomas's relationships with peers, curriculum, and materials converge, allowing Thomas to feel successful and become an active member of the community.

Thomas's Year Comes to a Close

Throughout the rest of the year, Thomas continued to have good days and bad days. Many of his successful moments occurred within the set of interconnected relationships he had built. And on the last day of school, Thomas did something he had not done all year while we were gathered in a community circle to share favorite parts of our year together:

Writer's Notebook Entry 6/28

Thomas asked if he could go first. This was a first for him, and the first in a long time for him to even share in circle. I felt I would cry then, but held back the tears to remember the morning's events. Thomas said Readers' and Writers' Workshop. Finally, we put in the *Let's Get it Started* CD. The children were in a circle, each going into the middle. I remembered back to when only about half the class would go in the middle. Today it ended up being all but one. The most rewarding moment of this was when Thomas chose to go in the middle and he was break dancing. Surprisingly, he took pride in his dancing. He was amazing. I thought that this ending might be the beginning of his next step in school and being a part of the community. I envision great things for him in the future.

When I look at this piece of writing, I see a celebration of the attention we gave to relationships throughout the year. The stories of Thomas's successes leading up to this moment demonstrate how all of the relationships Thomas built throughout the year led him to this day, to doing something he would not have volunteered to do in the past. Thomas's trust came from a year of opportunities to build relationships. He built relationships not only with his peers but also with readers and writers workshop—it had become a favorite part of his day. While most students would probably identify recess or lunch as their favorite, Thomas mentioned a part of the day when he felt successful, when he had peers to support him and materials he could use to express himself. Thomas's success reflects the idea of the "image of the child" as well as my belief in each child and the great possibilities for their futures. I always say that we "believe children into being," and this is what happened over time with Thomas.

Discussion/Implications

Thomas changed my way of getting to know children. He reminded me that I need to do everything possible to connect with each child so that he or she can reach his or her potential. Taking the time to observe children closely and letting the observations simmer as they fed thoughtful interpretations of literacy events led me to purposeful decision making. Though my decisions and actions were important, even more important was the time spent observing and learning about the various relationships the children developed, like those that allowed Thomas to experience success. During this year of teacher research—observing and using writing as documentation—I came to realize how critical it is to make relationships a *part of* the curriculum rather than a way to *get to* the curriculum.

Looking at relationships as part of the curriculum opens up doors for educators to think about the ways in which interactions occur within the classroom, allowing us to focus on relational decisions that can foster learning. In Figure 6.1, I summarize and give examples of this kind of decision making.

Relationships as curriculum is an idea valued not only by Reggio educators but by others as well. Skolnick (2000) discusses the idea of relationships in relation to literacy learning and posits the need to think about the relationships between children, between the child and the teacher, and between the child and

Data Source	Data	What Relationships?	Interpretation	Curricular Decision	Research Decision
Writer's Notebook	• Anecdotal notes used to create cooked notes	• Peer • Material • Curriculum • Time • Environment	• Bradley could encourage Thomas and learn from him. • Thomas was able to show procedures and share his strengths. • Friendship enabled success. • Choice in use of time and space allowed for success.	• Purposefully pair Thomas with Bradley. • Allow choice and open-endedness to give Thomas more entry points into the curriculum.	• Continue to focus on Thomas. • How are his relationships enhancing his participation? • Take time to write about this moment.
Writer's Notebook	• Anecdotal notes used to create cooked notes • Audio Recording • Photographs	• Materials • Peer • Time/Space • Environment • Curriculum	• Thomas's choice allowed him entry into the writing—this would not have occurred earlier in the year. • Rosie's purposeful choice of materials allowed a connection between her and Thomas. • Choice in use of time and space allowed for success.	• Continue to allow for choice in seating during this time. • Note the importance of materials in his success and see if it can be replicated in other areas.	• Use the photographs and audio to gain a better picture of the occurrences during this time frame. • Take time to write about this moment.
Writer's Notebook	• Anecdotal notes used to create cooked notes • Photographs	• Outside the classroom community • Material • Peers • Curriculum	• The girls gave a picture to Thomas that was created in Loving Care; they were thinking of him beyond the classroom. • His favorite items (stickers, books, grey marker) lured him into the activity again. • His friendships enabled him to be a part of the curriculum.	• Allow the stickers to be used in order to meet his needs at this time. • Listen and observe closely the interactions. • Allow peers to scaffold his learning and bring him into the day successfully.	• Take time to write about this moment.

Figure 6.1. Relationality chart for Jen's classroom.

the curriculum. My research group colleagues and I developed a conception of "relationships as curriculum" that consists of environmental relationships (materials, time, and space), interpersonal relationships (peers, teacher/adult, and community), and curricular/instructional relationships (curriculum, topic, and curiosity). Three key ideas about relationships emerged from this study.

First, viewing the environment as a teacher means thinking beyond the ways in which materials, time, and space can be used to enhance *each child's relationship* with the materials, time, and space. Giving them access to and choice of materials and free use of space is certainly important, but carefully documenting *how* a child uses these enables the teacher to make instructional decisions that support each child's learning. It is not enough to set up the environment for choice and access; the teacher also must be responsive to what the child is choosing. Using what we learn from children's relationships with their environment informs our decision making.

Second, it is essential to observe and take note of the interpersonal relationships that children have with one another. This adds a dimension to flexible grouping that we don't often talk about. Teachers often group students in their classroom by ability, interest, and/or product (Tomlinson, 2004). But another fruitful method is to be purposeful about the relationships between children by grouping them with those who will help them be successful. You can only do this when you give students the choice to work with others and then take careful note of their choices. Who are they working with and why? We need to start by observing, asking questions, and analyzing a situation before making thoughtful decisions about groupings and what constitutes success for a particular child.

These interpersonal relationships include the child's relationship with his or her teacher. The child–teacher relationship is strengthened through observation and interpretation; the more you to understand the child, the stronger the relationship. These interpersonal relationships can extend beyond the classroom if there is fluidity between home, community, and school. Children need to feel that they can share in the classroom what they are doing at home and in other areas of the community. At times this may mean dismissing common rituals and guidelines in the classroom to let life enter in. It means negotiating the curriculum so that children can be successful. This negotiation happened daily with Thomas; what became "allowable" for him was based on what he needed at the time.

Third, environmental and interpersonal relationships lead to building a relationship with the curriculum. A child's relationship with the curriculum must be a positive one for a child to feel capable of enacting the curriculum. For Thomas, the predictable structures of readers and writers workshops seemed to support positive peer relationships and encourage a love of reading and writing. Thomas did not willingly engage in these events early in the school year, but once he realized he was able to be successful through the materials he chose and the people he worked with, he came to love this time of day. I can only imagine that had we taught from a textbook in a more traditional format, his struggles would have increased rather than decreased.

It was clear from my notes that in the days that Thomas experienced success, all three of these dimensions of relationship were present. For Thomas, his relationship with the environment was always his first entry point into the curriculum. If he was able to choose his materials, as well as the location and order of his activities, he was able to participate in some way. Next were his interpersonal connections. Once he had the things that he needed or wanted for the task at hand, he was able to build stamina and sustain work because of his interactions with others. Together, his relationships with materials and his interactions with others led Thomas to be successful with the curriculum.

I learned from Thomas that I must observe a child's environmental, interpersonal, and curricular relationships in order to make purposeful decisions for instruction in the classroom. Throughout that year, I also learned that writing was the best way for me to come to an understanding of exactly what was occurring in the classroom. Writing was my window into the day, allowing me to think more deeply about the "why" behind the interactions in the classroom. I found that the more I wrote, the more responsive I could be and the more I understood what aspects of instruction would help Thomas and all my other students. Through writing, I was able to see the importance of relationships and all of the dimensions of those relationships.

Overall, this year taught me that I must believe in my students and the power of relationships in the classroom. For optimal learning to occur, it was important for me to sit back and allow relationships to take the lead. This meant setting aside personal comments such as, "I have so much to do that I don't have time to focus on relationships!" I realized that I don't have time *not* to build relationships. They are the core of teaching and learning, and they deserve to be part of the everyday curriculum if we want children to love learning and see the value in it. Relationships, when noticed, nurtured, and cultivated in the classroom, allow for more meaningful learning experiences.

Appendix

Layers of Writing

Writing was my primary method of making meaning of the relationships in the classroom. Here are the cooked notes I wrote after reviewing one day's anecdotal notes and the photographs I took, allowing me to re-create this particular literacy event.

January 18, 2005

On a shivering winter morning in January writer's workshop begins, the noise level is loud. Children busily walk to get the necessary materials: blank books, markers, crayons, paper, stapler, tape, etc. Thomas rushes to the collection of blank books and decides to choose a book where he can draw pictures and write words. He notices his friend Rosie, and sits down next to her. She sees the book he's chosen, quietly gets up, and walks over to pick up one just like it. On her way back she strategically selects a grey marker (Thomas' favorite color) and sits back down next to him. Their chairs are close to one another, so close that they sometimes touch elbows, shoulders, or their arms cross. They begin to author their own books. Thomas decides to make his own version of The Three Little Pigs *but mentions that he doesn't know how to write it. We begin to share the pen as I start to write with him and then ask what he hears in pigs. He states the P sound and writes it down. We finish this together. Then he writes his name. He decides he wants to draw the wolf but is not sure how. Rosie says, "I think I can. I'll try." He slides his paper to her as she places her hands gently on his book and pulls it close. She uses his grey marker and carefully draws the wolf. Her gaze fixated on the paper as Thomas is nearly shoulder to shoulder with her, his eyes peering at her hand drawing the wolf as if he's studying what she's doing. They continue to work together closely, eyes and hands busy. Thomas is not sure how to draw the door to the house. Rosie simply states, "Just make it like the T in your name. See that stick, it's just like that." Rosie used what Vygotsky (1978) would call scaffolding. Thomas then takes his grey marker and makes the door with a smile on his face. They turn the page and begin a new one. As they continue to cross space, Thomas points to his picture as she turns the page of the book. He looks at the Jon S. book closely, leaning towards it, tummy resting on the table and head up, eyes peering down, with his marker ready to write, barely lifted from the paper. Simultaneously, Rosie is working on her own version of* The Three Little Pigs. *Together they both complete books that are similar, but different. When Thomas finishes, he is ecstatic and wants approval to take it home. I ask if we can copy it first. He says "yes" and we walk down to copy his important work: his book—his writing.*

Next, I analyzed the notes to add a layer of interpretation:

January 18, 2005	Interpretation
On a shivering winter morning in January writer's workshop begins, the noise level is loud. Children busily walk to get the necessary materials: blank books, markers, crayons, paper, stapler, tape, etc.	*The start is always a little loud. Children can get their materials to begin—they know what they need—their writing folders and any types of writing materials that will help them in their work—understanding on what to choose and how it will help their work—relationship with materials and environment*

Thomas rushes to the collection of blank books and decides to choose a book where he can draw pictures and writes words.	First time he chooses this type of book. Choice in materials allows him to be successful.
He notices his friend Rosie, and sits down next to her.	Chooses a seat by his friend.

I then followed with an additional layer of writing to further define the event. Some of this writing you can see in the body of this chapter.

As I think about this piece of writing—it was another example of a chunk of the day that was completely successful for Thomas because he was able to work alongside a friend and had choice in what he was doing. Though every minute of the day he did not experience this success, I continued to learn from when he did experience success in order to think about the other parts of the day. As I read through this I am thrilled that he was willing to do everything and I think that is because he found a way to relate to what we were doing during this time and his friend Rosie helped him with that. Here the friendship and understanding of one another supported success. The relationships with materials again are very important—the kids know where they are, what to do and how to use them. They are then able to choose what is going to work best for them. Had Thomas been given the book he used today in the beginning of the year, he would have shut down, which was typical behavior when presented with something that was overwhelming or too hard. But here, he was able to choose that book and then use those around him to be successful. He was ready for it at that time and had not been prior. Giving the children access to a variety of materials enabled them to take the challenges they were ready for. Then, during this vignette, it is obvious that Rosie and Thomas have a special friendship and that she understands him. She knows he likes the color grey. She knows that he likes the 3 Little Pigs. She chooses to write a book similar to his and to sit next to him and even choose the same type of book. She was able to show him how to draw the wolf and then the next time scaffold the experience of the door, giving him an example of how it related to his name and then watching him do it.

As you can see, this layered writing process allowed me to make meaning of a specific literacy event. I didn't do this kind of writing right away or for every literacy event I witnessed. Instead, I selected a few significant events that I thought would help me understand the ways in which relationships assist in literacy learning. I used this layered writing process not only to understand the children's thinking but also to understand my thinking about children. It became a tool for reflection on teaching and learning.

Bibliography

Bissex, G. L. (1994). Teacher research: Seeing what we are doing. In T. Shanahan (Ed.), *Teachers thinking, teachers knowing: Reflections on literacy and language education* (pp.88–104). Urbana, IL: National Council of Teachers of English.

Cadwell, L. B. (1997). *Bringing Reggio Emilia home: An innovative approach to early childhood education.* New York: Teachers College Press.

Cadwell, L. B. (2003). *Bringing learning to life: The Reggio approach to early childhood education.* New York: Teachers College Press.

Calkins, L. M. (1994). *The art of teaching writing* (new ed.). Portsmouth, NH: Heinemann.

Calkins, L. M. (2001). *The art of teaching reading.* New York: Longman.

Collins, K. (2004). *Growing readers: Units of study in the primary classroom.* Portland, ME: Stenhouse.

Corsaro, W. A. (1985). *Friendship and peer culture in the early years.* Norwood, NJ: Ablex.

Edwards, C. (1993). Partner, nurturer and guide: The roles of the Reggio teacher in action. In C. Edwards, L. Gandini, & G. Forman (Eds.), *The hundred languages of children: The Reggio Emilia approach to early childhood education* (pp.151–170). Norwood, NJ: Ablex.

Edwards, C., Gandini, L., & Forman, G. (Eds.). (1993). *The hundred languages of children: The Reggio Emilia approach to early childhood education.* Norwood, NJ: Ablex.

Fletcher, R., & Portalupi, J. (2001). *Writing workshop: The essential guide.* Portsmouth, NH: Heinemann.

Fu, V. R., Stremmel, A. J., & Hill, L. T. (2002). *Teaching and learning: Collaborative exploration of the Reggio Emilia approach.* Upper Saddle River, NJ: Merill Prentice-Hall.

Gandini, L. (1993). Fundamentals of the Reggio Emilia Approach to Early Childhood Education. *Young Children, 49*(1), 4–8.

Hubbard, R. S., & Power, B. M. (1999). *Living the questions: A guide for teacher-researchers.* Portland, ME: Stenhouse.

Katz, L. G., & Chard, S. C. (2000). *Engaging children's minds: The project approach* (2nd ed.). Stanford, CT: Ablex.

Kincheloe, J. L. (2003). *Teachers as researchers: Qualitative inquiry as a path to empowerment* (2nd ed.). New York: Routledge.

Lewin, A. (1995). *The fundamentals of the Reggio approach.* Presentation to visiting delegation at the Model Early Learning Center, Washington, DC.

Lytle, S. L., & Cochran-Smith, M. (1992). Teacher research as a way of knowing. *Harvard Educational Review, 62*(4), 447–474.

Lysaker, J. (2004). Unpublished instructional materials.

Owocki, G., & Goodman, Y. (2002). *Kidwatching: Documenting children's literacy development.* Portsmouth, NH: Heinemann.

Ray, K. W., & Cleveland, L. B. (2004). *About the authors: Writing workshop with our youngest writers*. Portsmouth, NH: Heinemann.

Rinaldi, C. (1992, January). *Corso d'aggioramenti per nuovi insegnanti.* Address presented at seminar for new teachers, Reggio Emilia, Italy.

Sarason, S. B. (1982). *The culture of the school and the problem of change.* Boston: Allyn and Bacon.

Skolnick, D. (2000). *More than meets the eye: How relationships enhance literacy learning.* Portsmouth, NH: Heinemann.

Tomlinson, C. A. (2004). *How to differentiate instruction in mixed ability classrooms* (2nd ed.). Alexandria, VA: ASCD.

Wenger, E. (1998). *Communities of practice: Learning, meaning and identity.* Cambridge, UK: Cambridge University Press.

⊚ Research Conversations: Writing about Classroom Life as a Provocation for Reflection

WITH JENNIFER WHEAT

JUDY: It seems that in your research process writing was key. Can you talk about the kind of writing you did, how you got into it, and how . . . you think it helped you?

JEN: A lot of the writing started out as anecdotal notes, just quick notes during the day. I did it a couple of different ways. First I used a binder with sheets of paper where I wrote my notes. Sometimes I would type them up at the end of the day and print them out and put them in the binder alongside the handwritten notes. Then as the year went on, I got a spiral notebook and started writing the notes in the notebook. But I kept the binder because I had a tabbed section for each child, so when I had conferences with them I could also take anecdotal notes. Typically I would start out with anecdotal notes. Usually something would stand out. Then on Saturday mornings I would take the anecdotal notes that were pertinent to my research and "cook" them—add in my own thinking and flesh out things that I remembered about the event that might not have been in the original notes.

JUDY: Talk a little about that process.

JEN: I would pull up a file on my computer. Then I would read my notes and find those things that were pertinent to my study and add more thinking to what I had already written.

JUDY: So that's when the interpretations really started developing?

JEN: Yes. I did that throughout the year, most weekends. And during that writing I would often get new "ahas" and I would use them for the coming week in planning how to respond to kids.

JUDY: But that wasn't the end of how you used writing, was it?

JEN: No. The next part was taking the "cooked notes," the Saturday writing I had done on the computer, and revisiting it and diving in a little deeper. This extra writing would help me make sense of what was really going on with the children. Then I would sit back down with the other data I was gathering and write more to see what connections I could make between the interpretations I was developing in the writing and the other data. During this later writing, I also thought about how to make the work public, and that seemed to push me to analyze at a different level than during the early writing. So even though ideas would come out of the early writing, it was really going back and revisiting that writing and doing some coding that really brought those ideas along.

JUDY: It sounds like the idea of audience became important. When you start to think that someone else needs to be able to make sense of this too, then you begin analyzing at a different level in order to make it useful in that more public venue. So you have your initial writing, an initial interpretation, and then a more developed interpretation later on, deepened by more writing and another purposeful look at the data. You've hinted that this influenced curricular decisions and I would think data decisions as well. I wonder if you could talk about how this writing influenced how you thought about the children or your relationships with the children.

JEN: I think it really made me kind of stop and slow down a little bit. Just the act of writing things down gave me pause to think about what was going on with a child.

JUDY: You created a new space for yourself to think.

JEN: Yes. When I did that it would help me look at things with a different lens. So even though I would still sometimes find myself just reacting to what was happening in the classroom instead of thinking, it was less likely because I had my notebook there. I would just stop a minute and write. This would often be enough to shift my perspective.

JUDY: So the notebook was almost a provocation for you to be thinking constantly, just because of its presence.

JEN: Yes, and of course it really helped me notice things. I remember towards the beginning of the year seeing the relationship between Thomas and Bradley and how they could help one another in ways that helped Thomas be successful. But I think that if I hadn't taken the time to observe and write things down, to just notice how often they worked together and then take a closer look at that relationship, I might not have noticed how their relationship was building and how it was helping Thomas. I might have encouraged them to form other relationships or make different choices.

JUDY: So writing kind of gave you a history of your own thinking, and then when you viewed that history you could find the patterns that informed you as a teacher. You know, we often talk about the use of time, space, and materials from a Reggio perspective. It sounds like the notebook as a material thing created an affordance for taking the time and space you needed for thinking. Just having it with you seemed to invite a different kind of stance. I guess we often think about putting materials in the environment to be "provocations" for children, to inspire their thinking. We don't often think of the same kind of thing for teachers. If you were to give some advice to other teacher-researchers about writing, what would that be?

JEN: I think that finding a way that writing works best for your own personal style is probably the best advice—finding a system that works and trying things out to make sure that what you choose is really something you can and will come back to. Being able to come back to your notes is so important. That's how you make sense of things. And then of course make sure whatever you choose is easy to carry around!

JUDY: It's so interesting to think of this kind of writing—teacher research notebooks and journals—as ways that teachers create texts for themselves. We have so many texts that are given to us as teachers, texts that we're supposed to work with or pay attention to. Of course, scripted texts would be the most extreme example. But to have your own texts that you create to help you develop your own thinking seems like a very practical way to push back on some of the imposed structures that we have. Did your notebook writing help you in this kind of way?

JEN: I think the notebook writing became evidence of what was really happening in terms of the learning in my classroom, and I could use it in conversation with others. It also gave voice to the children and brought those voices forward. For me personally it helped me see that the children were benefiting from what we were doing in the classroom, that they were learning and growing. That was most important. With accountability pressures so high, I never felt like I was without the documentation I needed. If someone came and asked me about what the children were learning, I could go to my notebooks.

JUDY: Your notebooks became a place to find support for your own teaching. Often when we think of support for teaching, we think about it coming from other people, and we all know we need some of this. We need each other and a community. But you were able to generate support for yourself, which also seems pretty important.

JEN: Yes, and I think that the kind of support and evidence in the writing is especially important with the push to depend nearly exclusively on quantitative data when talking about kids and learning. Qualitative data, like writing, needs to be put alongside of all this quantitative data. Having qualitative data shows the more subtle kinds of progress that children make and the work of teachers. You can learn so much from this kind of data.

JUDY: Thanks, Jen. I think we'll leave it right there.

A Look at Cultural Tools in a Reggio-Inspired Kindergarten Readers Workshop

7

KRISTIN SCIBIENSKI

Just over two years ago, I joined my colleagues on a professional journey to incorporate writers workshop into our kindergarten curriculum. Inspired by *About the Authors* (Ray & Cleveland, 2004) and the excitement and support from colleagues, I introduced writers workshop to my students the second week of school that August. Later that month, I was invited to join a study group focusing on research and literacy and began to attend the Thursday meetings. As group members discussed their studies and research questions, I took on more of an observer role and found comfort in the community of learners. I didn't really have a research question or other goal, but there was something about our meetings that kept enticing me to return, something about the rich conversations and thoughtful silences, questions and hypotheses, and feelings of incredible respect for children and learning. Each meeting was one of those hard-to-describe experiences that touches your life. I was captivated. I immersed myself in writers workshop and began developing questions: How should my mini-lessons connect day to day? What was the best way to document conferencing? Should there be a structure to our sharing time?

I didn't have a specific focus at first, but I was deeply interested in our writing work. I came to understand that "[teachers] don't always start out with a specific, clearly formulated question. As observers of classrooms daily, we can unearth our questions by reflecting on what we see" (Shagoury & Power, 2012, p. 20). I began taking notes, collecting children's work, reading more about writing craft, and developing a writing habit—and eventually the questions emerged from the daily life of my classroom.

I began to study writers workshop in earnest and became overwhelmed with the amount of data I was accumulating. Once again I turned to our study group for support. We read through the notes and discussed patterns that seemed to be emerging. These patterns helped me to be more responsive and purposeful in my mini-lessons, literature selection, and talk about books. My research helped me show myself what I was doing.

I came to identify myself as a teacher-researcher and writer, and became more aware of the intimate connection between reading and writing. I now read with a different lens; whether fiction, memoir, articles, columns, my reading work had a different purpose. I even found myself listening differently, noticing well-crafted text in speeches, movies, and sitcoms. As I encountered the world around me, I became more conscious of how things were said, both as a teacher of writers and as a growing writer myself. As I reflected on children's work, it was clear that for them too so much of what they knew about writing had come from hearing it as a reader first. I began to wonder how readers workshop might naturally evolve from writers workshop with young children. And that is where I started the following school year. Inspired by my children's active inquiries during writers workshop, I wondered, *What does readers workshop look like as inquiry in kindergarten?*

My Classroom and Reggio Influences

I am a full-day kindergarten teacher in a large midwestern city. Like others who ground themselves in the thinking of our Italian colleagues (see Chapter 1), I value learning alongside our children, using observation as a tool to help me develop authentic instruction, and the role of relationships and environment in learning (Cadwell, 2003). As I set out to study how readers workshop would look in this environment and through this set of beliefs, I wanted to listen, watch, and learn alongside the children as they worked within the readers workshop structure. I wanted to be attentive and to document their activity, their talk, and their play. I consciously attempted to merge my inquiry into readers workshop with their inquiries so we could negotiate and construct our readers workshop as a learning community.

Establishing the Readers Workshop Environment

> It is organic instead of rigid. It serves a larger purpose. It is not neat and tidy; rather it reflects the complexity and order of the universe. It evolves; it is flexible. It has flow and movement. It honors the integrity of all involved. It is not imposed from the top; rather it grows out of a dialogic group working closely together. (Cadwell, 2003, p. 5–6)

These thoughts on the organization of the schools in Reggio Emily, Italy, are reminiscent of readers workshop in my classroom. Some days are quiet, calm, purposeful, and productive. Some days are loud and filled with motion and shifting intention.

Let me tell you how we started out. During the first few weeks of school, we spent lots of time with books. I introduced and read aloud a variety of books, including many of my favorites, and provided short periods of time for the children to read with one another. As a class, we began to organize our library and sort books that we had read together into labeled containers.

We talked about what readers workshop could be, based on our experiences with writers workshop. We began to develop a definition of readers workshop as a time of day when we worked on growing as readers. We thought together and talked about what we knew about reading: "Who do you know that is a reader?" "Where do you read?" "What does reading look like?" We used Post-it notes to sketch and record our reading memories, as described in *Growing Readers* (Collins, 2004). We used published books to do "detective work" and answer questions such as "What in this book reminds you of something else?" or "What do you notice about the punctuation in this book?" (Ray & Cleveland, 2004). Although in this way I was guiding children toward what I thought reading might be for five- and six-year olds, they showed me that they already had their own ideas.

Research Journal

"Teacher, Miss Scibienski, I brought my bunny book!" exclaims Brianna last Thursday. I am just as thrilled as she is, if not more. The day before, we had brainstormed reading memories. I started out by sharing an example from my childhood. I told them about how my dad usually read to all of us—eventually six—and how sometimes we couldn't understand the words because he would yawn right through them. I knew reading was important to him because even though he was tired, he still wanted to read with us. I told this story so that the kids would just start thinking more about reading. *Who do you like to read with? Do you have books at home? Do you have a favorite book?* I sketched my memory on a Post-it note first, and then sent them off to work. We collected our responses on a chart and shared them with each other. Brianna shared that her favorite book was "the bunny book" that her mom always reads to her before bed.

When Brianna brought "the bunny book" from home the next day, she created more common ground for us as a literate community. Because of her, we created a chart listing our favorite books from home and inspired others to bring in books to share, building that powerful connection between home and school. When Ava shared *One Fish, Two Fish, Red Fish, Blue Fish* (Seuss), she helped me remember that reading is like a performance: it takes lots and lots of practice, and audience participation is key. This is what happened:

> As Ava sits in the teacher chair, she reads the title, pointing to the words, and holds up the book for the kids to see. Chris asks, "Is that a long book?" "Yes," she replies. He turns back to look at me and says, "It's kind of a long book." Ava starts flipping through, carefully choosing pages to read to the class. "Look at this part," she says. 'Some are really skinny and some are very fat.' The class bursts into laughter. She chooses another page and holds up the book with her arms stretched high, making sure that everyone can see. "If you read that funny part again, we'll laugh louder this time!" shouts Samantha. And she reads it. And they laugh. And it is louder.

On a typical day in readers workshop, children would read with a friend, listen to an adult read, build word puzzles, talk about books, or rehearse classroom rituals such as playing teacher. As children invented and engaged in new activities, we talked about them as a group and decided whether they should be added as reading choices. We had ongoing conversations about what we could do during this time of our day and created documentation with photographs and corresponding descriptions to help children revisit these conversations. This became a cyclical process in which "an encounter between children and materials coincides with their imagination or interest [and] is recorded by a teacher or saved in an artifact . . . which becomes a provocation to pursue the encounter into the future" (Gandini, Hill, Cadwell, & Schwall, 2005, p. 53).

After a few months of exploring materials and experimenting with reading, children's inquiries began to shift and focus more on the print itself. From very early on, groups of children would spontaneously form around books that had been read aloud; being close to one another with stories seemed to be one way to get to know reading. But now as children built relationships with texts, with one another, and with the idea of reading, they began to expand their inquiries. They no longer interacted only with books—they passed out other materials such as pointers, alphabet charts, and paper to friends; used Post-it notes to mark their thinking and share connections they made; and took on the roles of teachers and students playing school. They experienced a sense of authority in having choices, becoming experts, and taking on roles.

Relationships with texts and tools built early in the year were supporting children in new ways as they grew as readers. One child seen in multiple photographs spanning eight months with the same book in front of him certainly had constructed a relationship with that text. How did he come to love that book?

Was it because the community had such an interest in it or because he wanted to learn how to read it? How did repeated interactions with that text promote his development as a reader?

As I looked over my notes and photos from those early weeks, it became apparent that particular aspects of our environment were pivotal to a child's learning during readers workshop. This led me to my next research question: *In what ways do children use cultural tools during readers workshop to support their reading inquiries, and how does their use relate to literacy development?*

Important Literature

I learned about readers workshop from the work of Lucy Calkins (2001), Kathy Collins (2004), and Cathy Mere (2005). Calkins and Collins draw a picture of the overall routine and predictable nature of readers workshop teaching—mini-lesson, independent reading and conferences, and sharing time—and emphasize the importance of community, access to materials, a print-rich environment, and opportunities for talk. These were all familiar to me from my work with writers workshop. Cathy Mere prompted me to think about the role of explicit teaching in mini-lessons and children's need for "practice time" as they learn strategies to handle print, genre, and the basics of how books work.

But it was Randy Bomer (2003) who got me thinking about the idea of "tools." He discusses the role of tools in primary writers workshops and the relationship between the use of tools and literacy development. I began to see, as Whitmore and his colleagues (2005) suggest, that children "come to know literacy as a cultural tool and a system of meaning making" through knowledge construction and participation in daily life (Whitmore, Martens, Goodman, & Owocki, 2005, p. 298), and to wonder how cultural tools might mediate reading development in my readers workshop.

Cultural Tools

Wertsch defines cultural tools as "any and all tangible and intangible objects" that support participation in and understanding of a specific culture (qtd. in Tabak & Baumgartner, 2004, p. 394), and Vygotsky tells us that cultural tools are resources in the community that act as mediators in a child's learning (cited in Haworth, Cullen, Simmons, Schimanski, McGarva, & Woodhead, 2006). So it would make sense that adults, peers, books, language, and other "objects" in our room might help children become readers. I found myself coming to a slightly different definition as I worked to study readers workshop from my Reggio-influenced set of beliefs. For me, cultural tools became *conditions of the environment* that supported reading development.

Reading Development

I thought hard about the reading development of five- and six-year old children as I watched my students engage in the beginning weeks of readers workshop, and I turned to Elizabeth Sulzby (1991) for help. Sulzby reminded me that emergent reading develops along a continuum and can be observed in children's reading of picture books. Her work is rooted in the following theoretical beliefs: (1) children are literate in the world long before they can read print, (2) emergent literacy is based on relationships with meaningful people and books, and (3) oral and written language development is simultaneous and ongoing. This perspective fit well with my image of the child as an active constructor of knowledge and my belief in relationships as an important aspect of learning.

I went on to read more about literacy development. Prisca Martens (1996) explains in her account of her daughter's literacy development that inquiries develop from children's perceptions that they don't quite understand something. This affirmed my commitment to watching closely to find the lines of inquiry as they appeared in children's use of cultural tools and to documenting the ways in which these inquiries led to their reading development during readers workshop.

The Study

I believe there are many ways to come to know things, and that knowledge is personal, social, relational, and environmental. I value knowing through experience, trial and error, conversation, and trust. I have found that engaging in inquiry and allowing myself to be somewhat vulnerable has given my students the space to see me as a partner in their learning. So I developed a flexible and broad plan for collecting and analyzing my data and did not try to distance myself from the data in some "objective" way.

I collected data on readers workshop for two years. My students made up a diverse classroom community each of these years, including Caucasian, African American, Biracial, Latino/a, and Asian students. The number of students fluctuated between eighteen and twenty-three due to the frequent moving of families within the district. Children with special needs and English learners were fully included and received support services.

Due to the nature of my question, I did not focus on specific children, but rather on the patterns of activity during readers workshop. My data analysis was ongoing and collaborative. As part of my everyday teaching and assessment, I took anecdotal notes and digital pictures to document student learning and regularly discussed these with my study group.

Data were organized chronologically in a large binder, and I kept a separate handwritten research journal. At least once every other week, I reread my notes as I categorized them by student. I then chose specific photographs and notes to compile in a research journal in order to use them to make connections to readings and to refine my questions (see the appendix at the end of the chapter). Photographs allowed me to look closely at a moment in time and possibly offer a new perspective. Through them I explored children's engagement, proximity, and use of space and materials. Community artifacts such as charts and documentation served as representations of literacy understanding.

I used coding to identify themes and patterns in the data and through constant comparison compared my codes across data sources and refined my interpretations (Hubbard & Power, 1993). I then triangulated data with the help of colleagues and members of my study group. During the research, I committed myself to writing and reflecting as a way to extend my thinking and develop new insights.

What I Found

It was difficult to decide how to talk about what I learned from my inquiry into readers workshop. My first inclination was to write it as a narrative, but I found it difficult to highlight the larger themes in this genre. So I decided to present my work here in a somewhat hybrid form: a thematically organized discussion of my findings enhanced by short narratives from my research journal. I intertwine my interpretations with the presentation of data.

The main themes that emerged from the data revolved around how children used the material resource of favorite books and the social resource of play as cultural tools within the readers workshop environment of our classroom. The use of these tools, motivated by their inquiry into the idea and practice of reading, helped the children develop their own "relation to the subject" (Palmer, 1993). See Figure 7.1 for an example of this kind of relationship, as well as a summary of the relationships that emerged as important in this study.

Data Source	Data	What Relationships?	Interpretation	Curricular Decision	Research Decision
Observation, Research Journal	Children's talk in which they ask for the same books again and again.	Children building relationships with particular texts	Children want to be able to find books they know and are developing preferences early, as they do with friends.	Organize classroom library and books with children's input and help.	Continue documenting children's preferences to promote relationship with texts.
Observation, Research Journal	Children start moving chairs around the room during readers workshop.	Children building connection to the processes and practices of reading	Children like to have control as they approach something that feels a bit out of their reach.	Stand back and observe while allowing children to incorporate play and manipulate parts of the environment.	Continue to document ways in which children mediate their own connections to reading through the familiar.
Observation, Photos	Child writes sight words on board for a friend to read.	Children extending and affirming relationship to the curriculum	Children re-create classroom ritual as understandings develop.	Share the experience in whole-group setting and talk about parameters for how it can fit readers workshop.	Watch for and document other ways in which children are inquiring into "how we do reading in kindergarten."
Observation, Photos	Children are putting books side by side and noticing words that are the same.	Children using relationships with favorite books and authors to make new connections to print	Children use familiar books to extend print knowledge.	Share connections with class and model one-to-one correspondence with print.	Continue to document other books that help children build print knowledge.

Figure 7.1. Relationality chart for Kristin's classroom.

Favorite Books as Cultural Tools

Favorite books that we read aloud became "shared objects" that connected children to the act of reading through revisiting and reenactment (Lysaker, 2000). Rhythm and rhyme and favorite authors were features of books that inspired their use and acted as mediating tools for children's reading development.

Rhythm and Rhyme

During the first week of school, we read, chanted, and moved to the rhythm of *Tanka Tanka Skunk!* (Webb). Upon the first reading, we were hooked; we became friends immediately. *Tanka Tanka Shunk!* had clear illustrations that helped us read the pictures, as well as repetition and rhyme and an overall movement that made it impossible to keep still. This was a book we connected strongly with and revisited for months to come. Because of our interest in this book as a community, it became a powerful tool for readers as individuals. Over the course of the year, *Tanka Tanka Skunk!* popped up in the hands of emerging readers time and time again.

During students' first encounters, they turned the pages quickly, looked for parts that caught their attention, and chanted the chorus in unison. The students' enjoyment was more about the rhythm and rhyme and overall sensory and social experience than about the actual reading of the text. This was a book that brought people together.

As children's experiences and interactions with literacy multiplied, their interactions with this particular text were altered. As Witte-Townsend and DiGiulio (2004) remind us, children "need to affirm through repetition what is known, predictable and therefore stable and comfortable" (p. 134). Then, when they acquire new knowledge about the reading process, "a tension between the new and the known draws children to revisit the same books over and over" (p. 134). Photographs and notes of children's reading showed me that their read-

Children Rereading Tanka Tanka Skunk!

ings of *Tanka Tanka Skunk!* became more detailed and precise. They were no longer just flipping through and browsing. Rather, with pointers in hand, children were deliberate and purposeful, paying attention to picture clues, beginning sounds, and text features. In anecdotal notes on March 16, I noted the following:

> Tommy and Damon have been in three different spots with song books (*Tanka Tanka Skunk!* and *If You're Happy and You Know It*). Tommy comes over pointing to the word "dingo" and says, "I forget what this is—I know 'donkey.'"

This is a very different interaction—one in which the children noticed print. Instead of chanting the comfortable refrain with each other, as they often did before, they were now tracking print, checking to make sure their spoken words matched the written ones, and conferring with peers when they were unsure. Multiple experiences with this favorite text helped move students along as readers.

Another text that became a favorite was *Down by the Bay*, based on the popular song by Raffi. As with *Tanka Tanka Skunk!*, the children's initial interest had to do with comfort. This was a song they knew. It was fun and silly and attracted interest from across the room. Children would gather around close together and sing in unison, laughing at the nonsensical rhymes: *"Did you ever see a fly wearing a tie? Down by the bay."*

As we focused more on rhyme as a quality of language and began to study word families as a class, students returned to *Down by the Bay* with new understandings. Tori and Mya were especially attached to this book and began to make lists of rhyming words and to copy portions of the text. Later, as they sang along, they pointed carefully to the now recognizable words in the book. The music and familiarity of the text became a stepping stone for these girls to make new connections to print and how words work.

These examples tell us that as children gain literate experience they return to books with different purposes. Although the materials—the cultural tool of the books themselves—were unchanged, readers used them differently as they redefined themselves as literate people. They came to the book with new curiosity to "reknow" it based on its history, their participation with it in the community, and their current understandings.

Authors and Illustrators

The second use of the material resource of books was children's choice of books by the same author. My students visited these books often over time, and the books provided familiar contexts for the development of new insights into literacy. A favorite author is like a good friend; in some ways, you know what to expect. Books by a familiar author provide a sense of comfort, predictability, and likeability. On the other hand, a favorite author, like a good friend, challenges your thinking and your beliefs. This seemed to be true for kids too. Children found comfort in seeing Eric Carle's signature, for example, or recognizing the style of David Shannon's illustrations.

How did they interact with texts differently after lots of exposure to a particular author's work? Here is an example from my research journal on March 26:

Field Notes
David Shannon's *No, David!* is a staple in our class. Everyone enjoys and finds comfort and humor in the simple text and story, especially on the page when David runs down the street without his clothes on. We have read a steady diet of David Shannon books all year and even designated a book tub for his work. The interest has been ongoing. However, after reading *Good Boy, Fergus* to the class a couple weeks ago, there was a new level of interest in his other books. The following day, Sydney and Brianna had *No, David!* opened up to the pants-pulled-down page, but not to get a reaction and laughs from friends, rather to point out that Fergus is in that book too. In fact, they searched the book tubs and shelves for all the books that had Fergus, or a dog that looked like him, in the illustrations. They even found a non-fiction book about dogs that had the same breed of dog shown on its cover.

David Shannon was a favorite author. In some ways, children knew what to expect. At the same time, his new book, all about a dog, caused them to shift their thinking and notice more in the world of books around them.

About a week and a half later, Sydney called out, "Miss Scibienski, I noticed something." As I walked over to her table, I saw that she had both *No, David!* and *David Goes to School* opened up to their final pages. "These are the same," she said, pointing to the words, "*Yes, David . . .*" at the top of each page. She had added yet another level of meaning to these David Shannon texts. Not only was she familiar and comfortable with the books as friends, but she also continued to gravitate to them as a challenge, attending to print and reading the words. In addition, she read to share her new understandings with the rest of our classroom community.

The children in my readers workshop were constructing new relationships with texts through familiar, comfortable older ones. And in some ways, all these relationships grew from our group experiences with books. Carlina Rinaldi's idea of "relational potentials" helped me to give this work more weight and to value the role of children's inquiries in this relational work (2006, p. 84).

Play as a Cultural Tool

In addition to the material mediation of reading through books, children used play as a way to develop relationships with the subject and the practices of reading. I describe three ways that children used this social mediation during readers workshop: playing with language, playing with the act of reading, and playing with reading practices.

Playing with Language

In exploratory play, children repeat an activity or skill again and again to feel good about mastering it (Owocki, 1999). This is one of the reasons that revisiting text is so important. Children experience satisfaction in returning to something familiar and trying to understand it fully. I am reminded of three books in particular that have been especially important in our readers workshop—*Tanka Tanka Skunk!, Five Little Ducks* (Beck), and *Down by the Bay.* Just as children use objects and materials to create a representation of something in their play, they begin to use familiar texts to create their representation of reading. As their understandings of the reading process shift, so does the role that the text plays. As children's experiences and encounters with reading grow, they return to the books with new purposes.

While listening, talking, and moving to the beat of familiar books such as those mentioned above, children internalized the language: "*Skunka Tanka / Skunka Tanka / Tanka / Tanka / Skunk.*" The patterns and repetition of rhythm and song books became part of who we were; Halliday (1996) tells us that children use language to build relationships and become part of a community.

"*And this is caterpillar. / His name has four beats. / Cat-er-pil-lar.*"

Then that rich, musical language in our minds begins to serve a heuristic function and becomes a tool for investigating and learning about language (Halliday, 1996).

As the children developed print awareness and made more and more connections to letters and sounds, the language of their favorite books allowed them to test out their thinking. In the case of *Tanka Tanka Skunk!*, as children continued to revisit the text, it became less about mastering the rhythm and more about mastering reading.

Playing with the Act of Reading

Lev Vygotsky discusses the notion "that people use external devices to regulate their behavior and to make thinking possible that would otherwise be difficult" (Bomer, 2003, p. 225). Cultural tools can change our understanding of the way in which we do something. Just as children used books as tools to make sense of something new in the complex world of literacy, they used play to set themselves in a knowing relationship with reading, making it feel less abstract, as noted in the following passage from my reading journal on February 8:

> Toward the end of Readers' Workshop on Tuesday a few kids started moving chairs over to the carpet. Last week, they had done something similar during Choice time and the row of chairs became the Polar Express. They were crawling underneath to load coal and connecting the chairs with math links. That time, it actually got a little out of hand. So … when the chairs started to appear, I reminded the kids—"You need to be making a reading choice." They assured me that they were, and started assigning people seats, saying, "This is the reading train!" and passing out books to kids that didn't have them. I stood back and watched the somewhat magical scenario play out. In a matter of minutes, six children were settled and engrossed in the books in their laps. I walked up and down the line watching them turn the pages, reading and pretend reading, more intently than they had the rest of the morning.

Playing with the arrangement of the room and adding an element of imagination made the complex process of reading feel a little more comfortable for

The Reading Train

the students. In describing the connection between play and language, Bruner (1983) identifies play as a medium for exploration and invention: "[It] is a kind of socialization in preparation for taking your place in that adult society" (p. 62). Corsaro and Molinari (2005) use the term *interpretive reproduction* to describe how children take part in and contribute to changing society. "Children produce and participate in their own unique peer cultures by creatively appropriating information from the adult world to address their own concerns" (p. 16). For many children, reading appears to be an activity from the adult world. As they begin to understand more and more about what reading is, they often become less confident in their ability to undertake such a task.

I am reminded of my student Maria and the many times she positioned herself somewhere in the room, book open and facing an audience, imaginary or real, engaged in the act of reading. She used a combination of knowledge, imagination, and the culture of our classroom to practice her understandings of reading. She played with reading by enacting parts of our day—chanting the ABC chart, choosing sticks with children's names written on them, and finding words in a story. In *Constructing Knowledge Together* (1992), Wells and Chang-Wells describe an event such as this as literacy learning through apprenticeship. Through demonstration and participation in the literate conversation surrounding our routines, the children "gradually [appropriate] the relevant behavior" in a social setting and begin to "take over more and more of the task" (147).

Playing with reading seemed to relieve some of the pressure and consequences of reading. Play made reading less serious if you didn't do it right. If we pretended that chairs in a line were a train, then when we sat on that train to read, we could still be pretending. If I pretend that I am a teacher and my friends are students, then when I read to them, I can just be playing. Play also offers both flexibility in and control of an activity that otherwise produces uncertainty. With the freedom to manipulate the environment, the children had a sense of control, which in the case of the reading train enabled them to create a playful representation that inspired diligent reading work.

Playing with Community Reading Practices

In many readers workshop classrooms, while children are involved in independent or collaborative reading work the teacher might pull groups to work on specific strategies. On several occasions, I worked with small groups of children, each with a copy of the same text, to practice print concepts and reading strategies, as described in *Guided Reading* (Fountas & Pinnell, 1996). Although this was not a consistent part of our readers workshop, it became a practice that children began to appropriate. On March 20, I captured the following literacy event in my field notes:

The boys rush over to the floor, each with a copy of the book, *Cocoons and Cases* (Wilson). It is obvious that Chris is in charge. He says, "It's called *Cocoons and Cases*." The boys seem to be re-creating a guided reading experience, although it feels like they are in fast motion. As they attempt to read in unison, the focus seems to shift to turning the pages simultaneously. On some pages, one strong voice is heard with echoes close behind. On other pages, the text is read in chorus. As soon as they read the last page, the boys jump up to trade their books.

"How about this one?"

"Where's *Good to Eat*?"

As Chris and A.J. comment about familiar titles, Damon patiently stands back awaiting the next book choice.

"Everybody get in a circle!"

The boys return to their spot on the floor and arrange themselves, this time with Chris sitting apart from the others. Again, they read in unison . . . very, very quickly.

In this case, in addition to the use of common texts, peer relationships were a huge support. Chris was a conventional reader, and he and Damon were good

Communal Reading

friends. Their relationship emulated that of older and younger brothers. Damon was trying to figure out his identity as a reader. He had a great sense of story and used lots of book language, but he hadn't quite made the connection between storytelling and the print on the page. He went back and forth between wanting to be part of a group and hanging around kids who were reading actual text, and being by himself and reading in a way that reflected his current understandings. A.J. and Brayden were very interested in print and had been making lots of connections with familiar words. By re-creating together the classroom practice of guided reading, each of the boys had the opportunity to take what he needed from the experience. Robbins (2005) describes such an experience of "mutual involvement, communication, and coordination of children and their partners" as guided participation (p. 145). By observing and then participating in an activity from the community, children are able to inquire into their own learning and construct new knowledge.

In the End: Reading Development and Space for Mediation

I'm trying to help Adam read because he doesn't know how. I got him the alphabet chart and he's finding letters.

—Karleigh, age 6

When I first heard Karleigh's comment, I was discouraged. I thought about all of the conversations our community had had about reading—things to read, places to read, different ways you can read, how looking at the pictures and telling a story is reading—as I tried to support each child on his or her own literate journey. But in retrospect, Karleigh's statement tells us a lot about reading development. As children encounter new experiences and test out and construct new understandings, their personal definitions of reading shift over time. Karleigh came to kindergarten with an image of herself as a confident reader and writer and would much rather draw and write than do anything else all day long. At this point in the year, she had figured out the relationship between print and meaning making and was very humbly (in a six-year-old way) trying to share that understanding with her buddy Adam. Based on her current definition of reading, he didn't know how to do it. Adam's definition was different. He was not yet driven by print in books. He knew all his letters and could recognize common words, but *reading* was about stories and connecting with people. Although Karleigh and Adam were at different places in their literacy development, readers workshop gave them the space and tools to support their growth as readers.

Just as painters study the craft of other painters and writers learn to write from other writers, we learn to read by reading and being read to. In kindergarten, children need to have the freedom to use the cultural tools of readers workshop to play with the reading process, supported by good teaching and quality literature. By building relationships with the people and materials around them, children are able to use the environment to scaffold their own learning. "In the end, though, as with a garden, the ecology of the whole takes over. Rather than making things happen, we become participants within an ecosystem that begins to bloom around us" (Cadwell, 2003, p. 33).

In negotiating the curriculum of readers workshop with my students, the workshop structure itself became a tool that allowed children to develop naturally as readers. As Bomer (2003) says, "Tools, in other words, point toward possibility, what is not yet, in order to take the user toward something new" (p. 245). I was a participant in the larger ecosystem trying to co-create time and space that allowed interaction with all kinds of literature and materials, opportunities for talk, play, and socialization. In doing so, children began to use tools—aspects of the environment—to develop mediating relationships with their own learning. This study showed me that favorite books could become a scaffold for children to try out new knowledge, and that the language and rhythm of familiar books and songs could provide comfortable places to build new relationships to the subject, in this case reading.

I learned that in play, children feel less inhibited and engage in activities that might otherwise be slightly out of their reach. They created their own scaffolds by re-creating classroom rituals such as forming a guided reading group or by arranging the furniture to concoct a reading train, making the complicated task of reading seem a little more manageable.

As children construct and participate in the reading life around them, they are changed by the new sets of relationships they create through inquiry—relationships with texts, with one another, and with the idea and subject of reading. This transforms the very nature of the classroom environment, making it a system infinitely more literate, more relational, and more responsive to the inquiries of all children. They are then able to approach new experiences with a sense of history and understanding based on the experiences they have helped shape.

In an age of testing pressures and accountability, when we are caught up in a discourse that favors academic achievement over the development of the child, it is easy to forget that children are competent and full of their own inquiries about the world and about language. It is easy to forget that if given well-considered access to time, space, and tools, children not only become competent readers but they also grow as people, as they make their own decisions about how to participate, learn, and develop in the world around them.

Appendix

Kristin's Research Journal

Connections to Reading

Constructing Knowledge Together (Wells & Chang-Wells, 1992)

> *"Talk in and about the activity can no longer remain an optional aspect of the collaboration."* (p. 147)

> *". . . involve contexts and activities that give rise to genres of language use in which speaking, listening, reading, and writing are integrated in order to purposefully engage in literate thinking . . ."* (p. 79)

When given the time, materials, and opportunity (workshop), children demonstrate and engage in the "activity" of reading. They are appropriating the activity, but the conversations and talk (about how and what and why they're doing what they're doing) help them understand the mental activity and thinking that is literacy. This reminded me of the importance of mini-lessons and sharing, and helping to "make big" the things that children are doing for everyone's benefit.

Connections to Children

3/30 Chris and A.J. are sharing the book *What's That Noise?* They are actually just holding the book in front of them, not reading or talking, just pointing to letters and words and following print. They get up to go get *The Itsy Bitsy Spider* book. With that book in front of them, they track the print, sing the song, and turn the pages.

Samantha says, "Miss Scibienski, I noticed something." She has *No, David!* and *David Goes to School* each opened up to their final pages. "These are the same," she says, pointing to the words "Yes, David" at the top of each page. Last week, Samantha and Ava searched the David Shannon books for illustrations of the dog from *Good Boy, Fergus!* She has been gravitating to these texts ever since, really attending to print and reading the words.

Bibliography

Bomer, R. (2003). Things that make kids smart: A Vygotskian perspective on concrete tool use in primary literacy classrooms. *Journal of Early Childhood Literacy, 3*(3), 223–247.

Bruner, J. (1983). Play, thought and language. *Peabody Journal of Education, 60*(3), 60–69.

Cadwell, L. B. (2003). *Bringing learning to life: The Reggio approach to early childhood education.* New York: Teachers College Press.

Calkins, L. M. (2001). *The art of teaching reading.* New York: Longman.

Collins, K. (2004). *Growing readers: Units of study in the primary classroom.* Portland, ME: Stenhouse.

Corsaro, W. A., & Molinari, L. (2005). *I compagni: Understanding children's transition from preschool to elementary school.* New York: Teachers College Press.

Fountas, I. C., & Pinnell, G. S. (1996). *Guided reading: Good first teaching for all children.* Portsmouth, NH: Heinemann.

Gandini, L., Hill, L., Cadwell, L., & Schwall, C. (Eds.). (2005). *In the spirit of the studio: Learning from the atelier of Reggio Emilia.* New York: Teachers College Press.

Goodman, Y., Reyes, I., & McArthur, K. (2005). Emilia Ferreiro: Searching for children's understandings about literacy as a cultural object. *Language Arts, 82*(4), 318–323.

Halliday, M. A. K. (1996). Relevant models of language. In R. S. Hubbard & B. M. Power (Eds.), *Language development: A reader for teachers* (pp. 36–41). Englewood Cliffs, NJ: Merrill.

Haworth, P., Cullen, J., Simmons, H., Schimanski, L., McGarva, P., & Woodhead, E. (2006). The role of acquisition and learning in young children's bilingual development: A sociocultural interpretation. *The International Journal of Bilingual Education and Bilingualism, 9*(3), 295–309.

Hubbard, R. S., & Power, B. M. (1993). *The art of classroom inquiry: A handbook for teacher-researchers.* Portsmouth, NH: Heinemann.

Lysaker, J. (2000). Beyond words: The relational dimensions of learning to read and write. *Language Arts, 77*(6), 479–484.

Martens, P. (1996). *I already know how to read: A child's view on literacy.* Portsmouth, NH: Heinemann.

Mere, C. (2005). *More than guided reading: Finding the right instructional mix, K–3.* Portland, ME: Stenhouse.

Owocki, G. (1999). *Literacy through play.* Portsmouth, NH: Heinemann.

Palmer, P. (1993). *To know as we are known: Education as a spiritual journey.* San Francisco: HarperCollins.

Ray, K. W., & Cleveland, L. B. (2004). *About the authors: Writing workshop with our youngest writers.* Portsmouth, NH: Heinemann.

Rinaldi, C. (2006). *In dialogue with Reggio Emilia: Listening, researching and learning.* New York: Routledge.

Robbins, J. (2005). Contexts, collaboration, and cultural tools: A sociocultural perspective on researching children's thinking. *Contemporary Issues in Early Childhood, 6*(2), 140–49.

Rogoff, B. (1996). Developmental transitions in children's participation in sociocultural activities. In A. J. Sameroff & M. M. Haith (Eds.), *The five to seven year shift: The age of reason and responsibility* (pp. 272–294). Chicago: University of Chicago Press.

Shagoury, R., & Power, B. M. (2012). *Living the questions: A guide for teacher-researchers* (2nd ed.) Portland, ME: Stenhouse.

Sulzby, E. (1991). Assessment of emergent literacy: Storybook reading. *The Reading Teacher, 44*(7), 498–500.

Tabak, I., & Baumgartner, E. (2004). The teacher as partner: Exploring participant structures, symmetry, and identity work in scaffolding. *Cognition and Instruction, 22*(4), 393–429.

Wells, G., & Chang-Wells, G. L. (1992). *Constructing knowledge together: Classrooms as centers of inquiry and literacy.* Portsmouth, NH: Heinemann.

Whitmore, K. F., Martens, P., Goodman, Y., & Owocki, G. (2005). Remembering critical lessons in early literacy research: A transactional perspective. *Language Arts, 82*(5), 296–307.

Witte-Townsend, D. L., & DiGiulio, E. (2004). Something from nothing: Exploring dimensions of children's knowing through the repeated reading of favorite books. *International Journal of Children's Spirituality, 9*(2), 127–142.

Children's Literature Cited

Beck, I. (1992). *Five little ducks.* New York: Henry Holt.

Haydon, J. (2002). *Good to eat.* Barrington, IL: Rigby.

Raffi. (1988). *Down by the bay: Raffi songs to read.* New York: Crown Books for Young Readers.

Seuss, Dr. (1960). *One fish, two fish, red fish, blue fish.* New York: Random House.

Shannon, D. (1998). *No, David!* New York: Blue Sky Press.

Shannon, D. (1999). *David goes to school.* New York: Blue Sky Press.

Shannon, D. (2006). *Good boy, Fergus!* New York: Blue Sky Press.

Webb, S. (2004). *Tanka Tanka Skunk!* London: Orchard Books.

Wilson, K. (2000). *Cocoons and cases.* Crystal Lake, IL: Rigby.

⦿ Research Conversations: Connecting to Big Ideas

WITH KRISTIN SCIBIENSKI

JUDY: I wonder if you could talk some about the ways in which you used writing as an interpretive tool in your teacher research work.

KRISTIN: I kept a research journal where I would write about what was happening in readers workshop. Then I would write to make connections between the literature and what the kids were doing. I would ask myself, "Where are the big ideas in all of this?" I was reading lots of different things and trying to write at least two or three times a week.

JUDY: So this was a way of thinking with your data and within a larger conversation with outside experts.

KRISTIN: Yeah, I was noticing some trends and things that kept happening in the pictures, and I would recognize ideas I had read about in the activity of the classroom. I'd find myself saying, "Oh, that's what she's talking about when she talks about playing with reading!" I was always trying to link ideas to my observations.

JUDY: Tell me a little about how taking photos entered into all this.

KRISTIN: I had taken so many pictures and reread some of what I had been reading, trying to think it through more. So this time around I did it all in one document; I inserted pictures and then started writing.

JUDY: It sound like you created a new physical space for yourself, one in which the concrete actions and intentions of your children in the photos and the abstract ideas you were working with could literally inhabit the same page facilitating your ability to connect the two.

KRISTIN: I think back when I first started I took so many pictures that it took me hours to print them all out and figure out what was really important to my questions. . . . [I]mporting certain photos, ones that really told me something about my focus, and then inserting a direct quotation from what I had been reading helped me *see the ideas in the photos,* which led to more thinking and the development of my interpretations. For example, I used photos to think about the environment and how kids transformed the environment during readers workshop.

JUDY: So the photo journaling, in the presence of the language of outside experts, really helped you to deepen your thinking about what you were observing. How else was writing important to your research?

KRISTIN: I think reading other things along the way just kept me writing, kept me thinking outside the box and making other connections that I wouldn't have thought of otherwise. I mean, I know that about myself, that I need to be reading a lot to be writing a lot. It's just like thinking about kids making books; it's always good to hear other authors' language and how they say things.

JUDY: Thanks, Kristin.

8

Our Pedagogical Experiment

JUDITH T. LYSAKER

All thinking is research.

—JOHN DEWEY

For two years, our teacher research group engaged in a shared curricular exploration. Grounding ourselves in a set of still-evolving understandings about young children and their learning, we investigated the ways in which readers and writers workshop curricula evolved in our Reggio-inspired, project-oriented early childhood classrooms. The studies that constitute the bulk of this book reflect each teacher's personal, specific enactment of this common general interest and describe individual inquiries into this larger multiclassroom "pedagogical experiment."

Each of us has developed personal insights about children's literacy development, the nature of curriculum, our own teaching, and the role of teacher research in our lives. These insights have provided us with information and inspiration for our work with children and have shaped our teaching in powerful ways, which we have shared in the preceding chapters.

However, our work has also informed us collectively, reshaping our thinking. It is these collective understandings that I address in this chapter. What we have learned falls generally into two areas. First, as a group of teacher-researchers, we have come to understand something of the specific ways in which the Reggio beliefs we embrace shape the way we and our students live out workshop. Second, and perhaps of greatest importance to us as teacher-researchers, we have developed a set of concepts about relationships from our examination of workshop through a Reggio lens. This set of concepts has deepened and extended our initial assumptions and has pushed us to consider "relationality" as the central pedagogical quality of our work. John Dewey (1938) tells us that learning comes from experience, that action leads to thought. This describes the way in which our new thinking came to be—through the daily actions of teaching and research, through ongoing reflection on the ways in which Reggio-inspired beliefs were at play in our work, and through the regular collective analysis of classroom data. Figure 8.1 shows this process. In the rest of this chapter, I first sum up the ways in which the Reggio approach to early childhood education meets and enriches the American approach to workshop curricula, and then describe how our studies pointed us to an overarching view of pedagogy and teacher research as relational work.

Reggio Meets Workshop

When we began our group inquiry into the workshop approach to reading and writing, we did not immediately see the ways in which our interpretation and enactment of these practices was related to the Reggio-inspired beliefs we held. In study group conversations, we focused on this set of beliefs more intently as we exercised them to understand workshop through teacher research. The following general conclusions come from this examination of connections:

1. Our image of the child led us to trust children as they engaged in workshop practices. This trust urged us to step back and observe, creating a new kind of space for the children and their work. We took up their thinking and their intentions in meaning making as mini-lessons. We watched and learned to value the negotiated coauthoring of written work, the co-reading of their favorite books, and the subtle presence of onlooking as a way of learning.

2. Our awareness of the power of the environment led us to cover the classroom walls with the children's texts: sticky note responses to books, dictated charts of their thinking, drawings, and documentation of the classroom in-

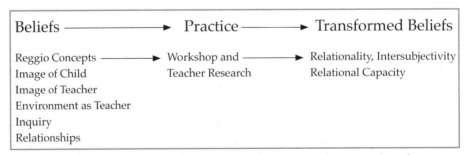

Figure 8.1. Relationships between theory and practice in our teacher research work.

quiries we pursued with children. Because we viewed these as representations of children's thoughts and feelings and not merely as decoration or some static record of workshop, we set up opportunities for revisiting and interacting with the children's texts around the room. The Reggio "environment as language" became a real idea for us, and we became keenly aware of the qualities of our discourse, such as tone and the sense of care made apparent through language, gesture, and body language.

3. Taking ourselves seriously as teacher-researchers made it possible for us to calm the day with the important research activities of observation, note and photo taking, and listening to and dictating children's talk. These less instructionally focused moments also created time and space for the emergence of children's thinking, inquiries, cares, and contributions. Workshop became a negotiated curriculum constructed and reconstructed by us with the children, a curriculum that became not readers or writers but literacy workshop. The lines between workshop and other parts of the day were frequently blurred by the provocations and representations of the children who perceived no disciplinary boundaries.

With these general conclusions about the connections between our Reggio beliefs and our experiment with workshop as background, I now discuss some particularly provocative junctures. These junctures are places where our earlier beliefs and the enactment of new practices pointed to something beyond merely an interesting alignment, places where a deepening awareness of our own beliefs emerged. In this section, I give examples of these junctures and focus on those that arose most forcefully in our studies and that perhaps best illustrate the ways in which our Reggio-inspired beliefs brought a new awareness of the classroom as a space most profoundly characterized by a quality of complex relationality.

Juncture 1: Image of the Child and Image of the Teacher with Independent Reading

As I mentioned in the introduction, our Italian colleagues speak of their "image of the child" as a central idea around which all teaching and learning are constructed. One's image of the child is essentially a set of beliefs one holds about children generally. *Strong, capable, active,* and *able* are all terms used by Reggio educators to describe children as learners. We embrace these descriptors and the beliefs they represent. In our conversations as a study group, we also use words such as *imaginative, open,* and *loving.* As our workshop practices unfolded, we found our image of the child slightly but significantly enriched as we thought about the child as *literate.* We began to see all of our students specifically as meaning makers who are creatively and actively in pursuit of literacy through inquiry, as well as engaged in co-creating the workshop curriculum with one another and with us. Our image of the teacher—most important, our view of ourselves as researchers—became more visible to us as our pedagogical experiment developed.

Kristin's view of the child as imaginative and resourceful allowed her to step back, observe, and trust the reading choices of children during readers workshop. As she tells us in Chapter 7, though making a "reading train" seemed on the face of it only tangentially related to reading work, Kristin paused, took photos, and wrote notes. Her role as a teacher-researcher, and her research question that focused on readers workshop as inquiry, gave her a kind of permission, as well as the tools that she needed, to allow children the time and space for the authentic, personally relevant pursuit of reading. What resulted was the use of play by children to make sense of the idea and practice of reading. As Kristin suggests, their construction of the "reading train," which consisted of children lined up in a set of carefully arranged chairs, could be thought of as an interpretation of what reading *was* for these children in this classroom. Reading meant that each child had a space to read (recall that some children were "assigned seats") and each child had a book (recall that some children were given books). Reading for these children meant that all sat at the same time together, in this case in the "train," but they spent time with books individually. Kristin remarks that in a matter of minutes, six children were settled and engrossed with the books in their laps.

Kristin's image of the child as a purposeful, active learner led her to respect the children's representations, be curious about their meanings, and give voice to those meanings within her classroom community. She posted children's "reading choices" for the community's later reference as they learned about readers workshop and about being readers. We see this as an example of what Reggio educators call the "pedagogy of listening" or "listening to thought" (Dahlberg & Moss, 2006, p. 15). Kristin was able to listen to her students' thinking and interpretations in part because she held an image of children as valuable in their own right in the present moment, not for what they will later learn or become. Her image of the child allowed her to notice and nurture children's sense of agency as people learning to read, as well as their burgeoning relationship with the idea and practice of reading. Children in a more traditional workshop structure, one less influenced by a strong multidimensional view of children and of teachers, might have been more quickly moved away from play into time with books more specifically focused on a new reading skill, strategy, or practice. Kristin's attention to how children used readers workshop to pursue their own inquiries about reading allowed her to see their relationships to the curriculum and to the idea of reading itself in a different light.

This juncture of our image of the child with independent reading points up the importance of the child's relationship with the curriculum—the course of action and materials provided for learning—and the child's relationship with reading, the focus of the curriculum.

Independent reading and writing were also influenced by our image of ourselves as teachers, in particular as teacher-researchers, capable of systematic observation and meaningful interpretation of classroom events. Patty's diligence in this role, which prompted her to take photographs of children regularly during their independent work, allowed her to capture the engagement of children during a difficult year. Despite the multiple challenges of children who had a wide variety of needs, Patty was able to review what was happening during the day and reconstruct her own understandings using the data she had gathered. As a result, she persisted in providing time for children to forge relationships with books and with one another during independent reading. Patty's image of herself as a knowledge constructor allowed her to see small groups of children meeting over texts, as well as the quiet child "looking on," as valid ways of building a peaceful community. In addition, through her research question concerned with children's relationships with one another, her research practice of taking and studying photographs changed *her* relationships with children. This juncture of our image of the teacher as researcher with the independent work of children illuminated the pivotal role of data collection in providing a way to establish, interpret, and nurture our relationships with children—and, more generally, all teachers' relationships with children.

Juncture 2: Images of the Child and Teacher with Children's Written Artifacts

In Chapter 5, Alyssa describes Mark's use of writing to connect to his family and how that connection was a context for his thinking. Mark brought his father's photographs to school and was eager to write about them during writers workshop. He began by drawing what he saw in the photos, then added a few letters and was ready, in Alyssa's words, "to pour out his story."

Alyssa noticed many things about Mark's writing. She noticed that Mark used the photos to connect with his father and with memories of their experiences together. She noticed that he used writing as a context for imaginative explorations of being powerful, and she asserted that this was part of his own construction of literacy. In this construction, home and school, as well as real and imagined events, came together in meaningful ways. Because Alyssa's image of children included a view of their activity in workshop as legitimately useful to them as learners, she did not disrupt Mark's representation of the photos in drawing. She trusted that Mark's drawing, an action he chose, was intimately relevant to the learning he needed to do at that moment. Because she trusted herself as a competent teacher-researcher, she listened carefully to Mark's story, constructing interpretations as she sat side by side with Mark, keenly attuning herself to *his* meaning making.

Alyssa valued and affirmed Mark's written artifacts as ways in which he was working toward an integrated sense of his life and of himself. Though Alyssa's research question had more to do with children's connections to materials, her ability to relate to the representations of meaning in Mark's written artifacts helped her to share in his meaning making.

This juncture of workshop and our image of the child points to the ways in which taking up children's work with the care and respect a strong image implies can build a teacher's relationships with children's written artifacts through shared meaning making.

Juncture 3: Image of the Child and Focus Lessons

Our image of the child often led to mini-lessons that were based on representations of children's thinking, presented to us through their play, writing, and talk. We regarded children's work as purposeful in its own right, reflecting the assumption that children contribute to and shape curriculum in important ways. As Malaguzzi (1998) put it, we proceed "in such a way that the children are not shaped by experience, but are the ones who give shape to it" (p. 86).

In Alyssa's classroom, for example, Sasha constructed a storybook in which she responded to her community's use of the word *hate*. This representation of thought, of moral purpose, and of personal concern was brought to the rest of the group at Alyssa's invitation and used to help the class think about how to work together and to provide a scaffold for their peers (see Chapter 5.) The children were drawn in by the unapologetic use of the word *hate* and honest reflection on the use of hurtful language. In writers workshop terms, the lesson highlighted the idea that writers write about what they know and care about. But Alyssa chose to let the author's intention rise out of group conversation, leaving the children with a lesson from Sasha that was Sasha's. This juncture between workshop and our image of the child made us more aware of the possibilities and purposes of our lessons, accentuating the child's relationship to the curriculum and to peers.

Juncture 4: Environment as Teacher—The Tone of Space and Time and the Materials in Workshop

When we think of environment from a Reggio-inspired perspective, we think of the use of space, time, and materials in classroom life. Each of these elements has physicality; space can be seen in the arrangement of furniture, the passage of time can be measured as the day unfolds, and materials can be touched and held. But we also know that these aspects of environment have less tangible properties. Space and time "feel like" something, and materials represent something beyond their physical realities. The junctures between our thinking about environment and our practice of workshop were pervasive and powerful. In this section, we begin by thinking about the qualities of environment needed for the sometimes very risky business of becoming literate.

Erickson (1987) reminds us that learning involves risk taking because it occurs on the edge of one's competence. To be on the edge of one's competence on a regular and frequent basis is an exacting personal experience (and sometime a scary one) that requires particular environmental supports. For us, these supports include a caring classroom community as well as the generous provision of time and a wide variety of materials to scaffold the risk taking.

In Chapter 3, Karen tells the story of Eric, a five-year-old English learner who came to her speaking only Spanish. He was a child on the edge of his competence in most things simply because he was a Spanish speaker in an English-dominant classroom. Blocks and the activity of building were important parts of Eric's day. This was clearly a place where he could feel capable as well as be physically and socially active in classroom life without having to speak English. Karen's commitment to making her classroom a place where children could feel valued, safe, and engaged led to a hospitable tone and open feel to her classroom. Her research question guided her to allow Eric to pursue his own inquiries into language, and thus she gained a view of the relationships he constructed with materials to support this pursuit.

In the Building Zone, Eric could create representations of his own imagination with blocks, alongside other children. As Karen tells us, building became inquiry for Eric, a way to articulate an imaginative stance about things in the world through the elaborate construction of towers. Building was also a way to inquire into literacy and the social world. It was within this safe environment, with the regular and generous provision of suitable materials (those that required no language), that Eric began to use English. Through signs such as "No Girls" and "No," he was able to gain control over language and build new kinds of relationships with his peers. Karen's acceptance of his Building Zone drawings during writers workshop supported Eric in moving from building with blocks to making representations of block buildings on paper, thus mediating his writing through play.

In this juncture between workshop and the idea of environment, we see more clearly the ways in which a hospitable environment, with a safe tone and the generous provision of materials and time, support children's relationships with materials and with peers.

Juncture 5: Environment as Materials and the Special Material of Text

The notion of the environment as teacher played out in especially provocative ways as we thought about text. First, text took on the role of "teacher." Margaret Meek (1987) addressed this idea primarily in terms of what text structures could teach a young child learning to read. However, for us "text as teacher" came to have a slightly different meaning. Texts, as *representations of others* in language, spoke to the children in ways that we as their teachers could not. Texts had their own, very different voices, personalities, and language qualities. Books became mentor texts (Ray & Cleveland, 2004), as they are often used in writers workshop, but in ways that went beyond mentoring children into a particular kind of writing craft or reading strategy. Text became another kind of relational space, which did two important things. First, books provided a vicarious social world for exploring, and second, books provided a kind of neutral, shared social context within which children could build relationships with one another.

Patty's work demonstrates the special power of the material of text. An enlarged version of *The Three Little Pigs* quite physically became a shared space around which children gathered. More than that, the language of the text, which they had come to know well from prior readings, became a shared language, one that could be voiced in unison by the children, who, Patty tells us, did not usually choose to be together in respectful, cooperative ways. Patty's careful book choices and continual revisiting of favorites with the whole group gave her students a discursive space they could share. This space was composed in large part of the words of books rather than their own words, which for whatever reason often left them at odds with one another. When children were engaged in the qualities of this particular kind of material—the language, the characters, the sense of connectedness to something beyond the here and now—that engagement, or relationship with text, was able to override the difficulties of that here and now. We think of this as children's relationship to the "subject" of reading. Parker Palmer (1983) suggests that the connective core of all our relationships is the significant subject itself—the power of the living subject. This particular juncture of environment and "materials as teacher" helped us to notice the special role of text in mediating children's relationships with one another as well as their relationships with their developing ideas about the experience and purpose of the subject of reading.

Another example of the special material of text in our environments was the use of documentation. Our documentation consisted of large, carefully designed panels filled with evidence of children's learning. We regularly posted in our classrooms this evidence of ongoing activity and learning in images, photos, transcriptions of children's talk, and our own short written reflections. In addition, encouraged by readers workshop advocates like Kathy Collins (2004), we eagerly created charts of reading strategies and lists of favorite places to read. As a study group, our Reggio background led us to view these environmental texts as "teachers," which fit well with notions such as creating a literate environment. Children's use of documentation and of other autobiographical texts went beyond remembering words, strategies, or events. Interaction with documentation and other autobiographical texts seemed to help children develop a relationship with themselves, a way to know themselves through the representations of themselves (texts) that they had created. In this way, documentation highlights the special *relationships between a child and him- or herself*.

Amanda and Kristin used autobiographical charts as part of workshop and project work. Kristin's list of children's reading choices, created from group conversation and then posted in the classroom at children's eye level, gave her students a view of their thinking as individuals as well as a community. In addition, their rereading of the list reminded them not only of the purposes and expectations of workshop, but also of their own *thinking* and how it was related to other people's thinking. Amanda's posting of children's questions about bugs provided a similar opportunity for each child to view his or her own thinking in relationship to the community. Each question represented that child's inquiry into the topic. The articulation of this inquiry—particularly in the somewhat permanent mode of writing—sets the child in relation to the subject, which he or she can view, interpret, and respond to.

Making Sense of the Junctures between Reggio and Workshop: A Model of Relationality in Early Childhood Literacy

> Knowing is inevitably practical. It changes the known.
>
> —Sartre

As demonstrated, our consideration of the junctures between our original Reggio framework and our new pedagogical experience of workshop led us to review and reenvision our earlier thinking about the role of relationships in the classroom. While we were already aware of the importance of relationships, our collaborative research changed, as Sartre suggests, what we already knew. Whereas relationships were once one of many ideas in a set of ideas, now relationships became the conceptual core, the place where all our work came together, and the place from which our new understandings would emanate.

Kinds of Relationships

For us, the ecosystem of complex relationships that is the classroom consists of three kinds. First are the social relationships, both inter- and intrapersonal. Interpersonal relationships are the teacher's relationships with children and the children's relationships with one another. The intrapersonal relationships consist of the child's relationship with him- or herself and the teacher's relationship with him- or herself. Second is a set of curricular relationships: the teacher's relationship to the curriculum and to the subjects of that curriculum more specifically, as well as the children's relationships with the curriculum and individual subjects. Last is a set of environmental relationships: the children's relationships with the environment and with the materials in the environment, as well as the teacher's relationship with these same things.

Articulating the kinds of relationships that we experience in classrooms is only the beginning of understanding the ways in which they are involved with learning. Having a sense of what constitutes relationships, what happens within them, and how they function as a whole within classroom life can contribute to that understanding. Our consideration of the junctures between Reggio and workshop has helped us to develop our thinking about these aspects of classroom relationships. In the following section, I briefly address these aspects and describe the idea of relationality and the consequence of this idea for our lives in early childhood classrooms.

Intersubjectivity

The essential quality of the relationships that have emerged as important in our work is one of *intersubjectivity.* Intersubjectivity occurs in relationships in which meanings are shared and in which there is, as Bruner (1986) says, a meeting of the minds—and, we would add, a meeting of the hearts as well. A central quality of intersubjectivity is therefore dialogic: it occurs because of a dialogue between the meanings of different people. As such it depends on the emergence of subjectivities (Rinaldi, 2006). For us this means that the conversations of intersubjective experience are contingent on a kind of "coming forth" of personhood, the surfacing of the child's real presence in the classroom.

Intersubjective relationships are sites of learning (Vygotsky, 1978). During intersubjective relational moments, self and other come together in a potent dialogic exchange that shapes the meaning making and the being of each child and teacher in the exchange. For example, when Alyssa interpreted the meaning in Mark's writing, she was working to share in his meaning making, to establish an intersubjective relationship within which they both could work. She was able to experience the personhood he represented—a young boy striving to connect his home and school experiences. This led Mark to value his own authoring and, we might argue, feel a sense of wholeness when his home experiences were so well understood and valued at school. Karen also provided an example of establishing shared meaning making when she resisted a more conventional interpretation of Eric's block building and allowed this expression of his subjectivity to emerge and develop. By taking up his meanings, she was able to support his efforts to express himself as a new language learner. Through her care of him, she established a "meeting of the minds."

Intersubjectivity also occurs between children. In Chapter 6, for example, Jen described Rosie and Thomas's joint construction of a version of *The Three Little Pigs.* The children shared space and materials as they wrote together, Rosie taking the lead in establishing shared meaning making through materials. Rosie noticed the small blank book Thomas had chosen for writing and quickly went to get one just like it, sending Thomas the message that "we are in this together." She then provided him with his favorite color marker. Jen described the two sharing materials within close proximity, jointly constructing a story.

An interesting example of intersubjectivity is found in one's relation to a "subject." How, in fact, does a teacher, for example, have an intersubjective relationship with reading? In Chapter 4, Patty discussed her particular relationship with the idea of reading aloud to children. Reading aloud had a particular set of meanings for Patty that she constructed through her own experience; it brought her peace and a sense of contentment. She demonstrated her relationship to the subject of reading every time she read aloud to her students. Her passion for books, her understanding of the meaning of reading in people's lives and of what reading might do for them, was all part of that relationship. As Palmer (1983) tells us in speaking of himself as teacher, "I teach more than a body of knowledge or set of skills. I teach a mode of relationship between the knower and the known, a way of being in the world" (p. 30). As teachers we demonstrate ways of constructing meaningful relationships to the known and to what we are trying to know.

Shared meaning making, or intersubjectivity, can also be established between a child and representations in the environment. If we consider that texts, photos, drawings, and so on are all representations of people, then each is an expression of subjectivity. When we take up the meanings of those representations and make sense of them ourselves, we have shared meaning. For example, in Chapter 7, Kristin charted children's "reading memoirs," which were displayed in the classroom at eye level in their large-group community space. This charting of individual children's words in a shared space was an articulation of a set of subjectivities. Children now could revisit what they had said or what a peer had said and make connections between the meanings of their reading experiences. Such a practice sets up the possibility of multiple intersubjective relationships. Though not exactly like the intersubjective experiences established between people in real time, these experiences with the representations of people offer new possibilities for understanding others.

The Role of Inquiry and Care

Inquiry is the basis of our own relationships and of our roles as facilitators of children's relationships. Inquiry might be best thought of as a relational stance characterized by an outward motion toward others and the world, a move from self to connection with "otherness," made possible by a hospitable, caring environment and inspired by the human desire to connect and to belong. An inquiring stance on the part of a child involves the *articulation of subjectivity* through meaning making practices. Through talk, play, drawing, reading, and writing, the child's subjectivity emerges into a set of intersubjective relationships that *is* classroom life. Intersubjectivity, then, is the quality of the relationships we form in our process of inquiring about one another and the world.

The ongoing presence of care on the teacher's part precedes and fosters the relationality of the classroom *by making inquiry possible*. Our classrooms are a set of layered, transactional inquiries. Foremost are the children's inquiries, both those of the community and those of individual children. Then there are the teacher's inquiries, both the larger inquiries she makes into her work, like those we have explored here, as well as the more intimate inquiries she has about individual children's lives and learning. We see these sets of inquiries as necessarily and beautifully interdependent, an ecosystem of our attempts to know, love, and understand the world and the people around us. The points at which the teacher's and the children's inquiries intersect are those most full of learning potential. Here the quest for knowing and for connecting on the part of the teacher and the children meet. In this overlapping of inquiries is a spirited energy and profound attentiveness that comes from intense focus and desire. The act of teacher research, in which teachers pursue personally meaningful questions, promotes the possibility of these intense, rich, and rewarding learning moments for both teachers and children. We have come to compare the role of the teacher-researcher to that of loving artist who observes and orders time, space, materials, and activity in ways that promote the establishment and sustenance of relationships on a daily and even moment-to-moment basis.

Curriculum as Relationality

We consider the whole of these relationships, what we are calling "relationality," to define curriculum. That is, curriculum might be thought of as the living out of a complex set of intersubjective relationships within a community. The relationality, the curriculum, of a classroom is complex and dynamic; it has both texture and motion. It is constructed and represented by meaning making and the inquiry that prompts that meaning making. The idea of relationality suggests an overlapping and intersecting of relationships across time and space that results in organic wholeness. The richness of this relationality depends on us as teachers valuing relationships in our classrooms as they evolve, from past to present to those we are imagining and envisioning. The relationality of a classroom is fostered in part by generosity and hospitality, which include the teacher's openness to the forging of relationships; his or her provision of appropriate space, time, and materials; and the ongoing careful and caring observation, interpretation, and documentation of the evolution of relationships.

From our work, we know that all relationships in our classroom have "intersubjective potential." This intersubjective potential is realized when we lovingly enter into the meaning making of children and when children are able to receive and respond to this kind of care. It is realized when we create physical and discursive environments that support meaning making. Finally, through our work, we have come to reframe the notion of inquiry as a *relational stance* children can take toward the people, the environment, and the texts of the classroom. In this way, the intersubjective potential of any classroom moment is also realized through inquiry.

So What?

One might legitimately ask why this way of thinking about early childhood curriculum matters. What are the ramifications of a relational approach to pedagogy and curriculum? Our work suggests a few answers to this important question. First, when relationality is the focus of the way we think about "outcomes," schooling changes. Academic success takes a backseat to "becoming" or "self-authorship." Competition is replaced by collaboration. The accumulation of skills is subordinated to the making of meaning. Community and the "common good" replace independence and individual gain. We argue that all of these outcomes will serve children well as they navigate a complex, global society.

Perhaps most important is that when teachers create, notice, and nurture relationality as a primary teaching goal, children develop "relational capacity," the capacity for connection to others and to their world (Lysaker, Tonge, Gauson, & Miller, 2011; Lysaker & Furuness, 2012). This capacity opens up largely unspoken relationships with *possibility*, with personal and communal histories and with personal and communal stories. To know and understand oneself, one's place in a community, to know something of what has come before and to glimpse something of the possibilities for oneself and one's community, something beyond the here and now—these are things that matter. These achievements, if we dare call them that, allow us to live in fully human ways. What more could we want from schooling?

Bibliography

Bruner, J. (1986). *Actual minds, possible worlds*. Cambridge, MA: Harvard University Press.

Collins, K. (2004). *Growing readers: Units of study in the primary classroom*. Portland, ME: Stenhouse.

Dahlberg, G., & Moss, P. (2006). Introduction: Our Reggio Emilia. In C. Rinaldi, *In dialogue with Reggio Emilia: Listening, researching and learning* (pp. 1–22). New York: Routledge.

Dewey, J. (1938). *Experience and education*. New York: Macmillan.

Erickson, F. (1987). Transformation and school success: The politics and culture of educational achievement. *Anthropology and Education Quarterly, 18*(4), 335–56.

Lysaker, J. T., & Furuness, S. (2012). Space for transformation: Relational, dialogic pedagogy. *Journal of Transformative Education*, 9(3), 183–197.

Lysaker, J. T., Tonge, C., Gauson, D., & Miller, A. (2011). Reading and social imagination: What relationally oriented reading instruction can do for children. *Reading Psychology*, 32(6), 520–566.

Malaguzzi, L. (1998). History, ideas, and basic philosophy: An interview with Lella Gandini. In C. Edwards, L. Gandini, & G. Forman (Eds.), *The hundred languages of children: The Reggio Emilia approach—advanced reflections* (2nd ed., pp. 49–97). Greenwich, CT: Ablex.

Meek, M. (1987). *How texts teach what readers learn*. Stroud, UK: Thimble Press.

Palmer, P. J. (1983). *To know as we are known: A spirituality of education*. San Francisco: Harper and Row.

Ray, K. W., & Cleveland, L. B. (2004). *About the authors: Writing workshop with our youngest writers*. Portsmouth, NH: Heinemann.

Rinaldi, C. (2006). *In dialogue with Reggio Emilia: Listening, researching and learning*. New York: Routledge.

Vygotsky, L. S. (1978). *Mind in society: The development of higher psychological processes*. Cambridge, MA: Harvard University Press.

Index

documentation for, 81
Cullen, J., 121
Cultural tools, 121–22, 124, 128–32
    defined, 121
    favorite books as, 124
    play as, 128–32
Curriculum
    children's decision making in, 96, 108
    daily routine and, 81
    inquiry approach to, 5
    making connections across, 80–90
    open-ended, 96
    predictability in, 96
    as relationality, 151–52
    relationships as part of, 107, 108–9,
      151–52
Curtis, D., 80

Dahlberg, G., 1, 8, 142
Danyi, D., 11
Da Ros-Voseles, D., 11
Data collection, x, 4, 12
    coding and, 123
    for cross-curricular connections, 82
    forms of data, 12, 82
    on language learning, 33–34
    on read-alouds, 60–61
    on readers workshop, 122–23
Developmental play theory, xvii
Dewey, J., 2, 139
DiGiulio, E., 125
Documentation, 3–4, 8, 94, 95
    anecdotal note-keeping, 47, 51–55
    of children's talk, 25–30
    children's use of, 147
    data analysis, 61–62, 91–93
    of language learning, 33–34
    organizing, 51–55, 61–62, 123
    of read-alouds, 60–62
    as teacher research, 44, 60

Ecotone, ix
Edge effect, ix
Edwards, C., 81, 96
English language learners, 33–43
    reluctance to participate of, 35

Environment
    arrangement of, 57, 80
    child-centered, 12
    children's relationship with, 108
    materials and, 145–47
    provoking thinking and creativity
      with, 80
    for readers workshop, 118–21
    space and time in, 145–46
    as teacher, 2, 4–5, 11–12, 57, 80–81, 140,
      145–46
Erickson, F., 145

Field notes, 97
Flaxman, S. G., 24
Fletcher, R., xiv, 94, 96
Focus lessons, image of child and, 144–45
Forman, G., 81, 96
Fountas, I. C., 32, 130
Fox, M., 58
Fraser, S., 83
Free play, 81
Fu, V. R., 96
Furuness, S., 152

Gallas, K., xiv, 4, 35, 58
Gandini, L., 5, 81, 94, 96, 104, 120
Gardner, H., 2
Gauson, D., 152
Gestwicki, C., 83
Goldstein, K. K., xiii, xvii
Goodman, Y., 97, 121
Greene, M., 46

Halliday, M. A. K., 128
Hankins, K., 4, 12, 71
Harste, J. C., 6, 35
Hatch, J. A., 11
Haworth, P., 121
Hildebrand, H., xvii
Hill, L. T., 96, 120
Hodgkins, F., 19
Home–school connections, 87–88, 103,
  104
Horan, P. D., xiii, xvii
Hubbard, R., 4, 58, 97, 98, 123

as cultural tool, 128–32
free, 81
with language, 128
as learning tool, xvii, 11
marginalization of, 11
as provocation to learning, 22
with reading, 128–30
Pontecorvo, C., 89
Portalupi, J., 94, 96
Power, B., 4, 58, 97, 98, 117, 123
Predictability, in curriculum structures, 96
Professional development, through collaboration, xv
Projects, 5–6, 12–24, 81, 94
children's inquiry through, 5–6, 12
incorporating play in, 12–24, 81

Raffi, 126
Ray, K. W., xvi, 6, 7, 32, 35, 58, 81, 94, 96, 117, 119
Read-alouds, 58–73
building relationships with, 58–73
children's use of, 62–63
context for, 59–60
record keeping of, 60
research strategies for, 60–61
shared language and, 62–63
Readers workshop, xvi, 96, 118–34. *See also* Literacy workshops
collection of data on, 122–23
cultural tools and, 118–34
developing definition of, 119
establishing environment for, 118–21
relationships in, 124
research literature on, 121–22
typical day in, 120
Reading development, 122, 132–33
Reggio Emilia approach, 1–11
basic tenets of, 1–6, 57–58, 94
commitment to, xv–xvi
enacting literacy workshops using, xvi
environment as teacher in, 45, 11, 140
historical and political contexts of, 1
image of child in, 3, 11, 57–58
inquiry approach to curriculum in, 5–6
as pedagogical experiment, 8–9

research on, 57–58
teacher role in, 3–4, 58
Relationality, xviii, 8, 22, 23, 39–42, 68–69, 70, 83, 123, 148–52
building capacity for, 39–42, 68–69, 70
curriculum as, 151–52
Relational pedagogy, xviii
Relationships, xiii–xiv, xvii, 6, 8, 94
care in, role of, 150–51
centrality of, 44–45, 102, 139
among children, 83–87, 108, 134
child–teacher, 108
classroom context for, xvii, 95–96
as curriculum, 107–8
documenting, 82
inquiry in, role of, 150
intersubjectivity in, 149–50
kinds of, 148
making cross-curricular connections through, 80–90
with materials, 83–88, 128, 134
with peers, 83–87
in readers workshop, 124
role in literacy environments, xiii–xiv, xvii, 6, 8, 44–45
shared meaning making and, 63–69
teacher research into, 95–111
with texts, building, 37–39
between theory and practice, 140
trends in, 82
Research, ix, xiii
focus of, ix
in literacy workshop, 12, 19
literature, 8–9, 57
writing component of, 97–98, 110–11, 114–16
Research conversations, xvi
on analyzing data, 91–93
on anecdotal note-keeping, 51–55
on classroom talk, 25–30
on connecting big ideas, 137–38
on photo journaling, 76–78
on writing to provoke reflection, 114–16
Research journals, 4, 82, 137
Rhythm and rhyme, 62, 124–26
Rinaldi, C., xiv, 2, 8, 44, 45, 80, 104, 127,

149

Rogers, H., 19

Sarason, S. B., 95
Schimanski, L., 121
Schomp, V., 19
Schwall, C., 120
Scibienski, K., xvii
Seating, children's choice of, 102
Sendak, M., 62, 63
Seuss, Dr., 119
Shagoury, R., 117
Shannon, D., 38, 42, 62, 127, 134
Shared language, 62–63
Share time, 7
Short, K. G., 10, 45
Sign making, 40
Sill, C., 13
Simmons, H., 121
Skolnick, D., xviii, 6, 95, 96, 107
Smith, F., 39
Snyder, W. M., 89
Social constructivist learning theory, 2, 8, 80
Stille, D., 19
Stremmel, A. J., 96
Student artifacts, 12
Sulzby, E., xvi, 122

Tabak, I., 121
Teacher
    engagement through research, 2
    image of, 43–44, 58, 95, 143
    preparedness of, 56–57
    as researcher, x, 3–4, 43–46, 58, 96, 118–19, 141, 143
    as theorist, 4
    transformative role of, xiv
Teacher inquiry group, xiv, 97, 139–40

collective understandings of, 139–40
Teacher research, x, 94, 95, 96–97, 117–18
    cycle of, 97
Text, 37–39, 146–47
    building relationships with, 37–39
    special power of, 146–47
    as teacher, 146
Theorist, teacher as, 4
Tomlinson, C. A., 108
Tonge, C., 152

Vocabulary development, 22
Vygotsky, L. S., 2, 6, 8, 89, 121, 128, 149

Wadsworth, R., 58
Webb, S., 124
Wells, G., 130, 134
Wenger, E. C., 89, 97
Westcott, N. B., 62
Wheat, J., xvii
Whitmore, K. F., 121
Witte-Townsend, D. L., 125
Wood, A., 62
Woodhead, E., 121
Wright, J. R., 13
Writers workshop, xvi, 36–37, 117–18. *See also* Literacy workshops
    building as authoring in, 36–37
    teacher research on, 117–18
Writing
    audience consideration in, 114
    image of child and, 143–44
    as interpretive tool in research, 137
    layers of, xvii, 98, 110–11
    as provocation for reflection, 114–16

Zone of proximal development, 8
Zuehlke, J., 19

Editor

J udith T. Lysaker is an associate professor of literacy and language education at Purdue University. She taught first grade for five years before receiving her doctorate from Indiana University in language education. Her research and publications have focused on relational aspects of teaching and learning, as well as on reading as a dialogic, relational process that influences the development of children's social imagination. Lysaker is currently exploring developmental differences in young children's uses of social imagination during wordless book reading.

Contributors

Amanda Angle has been a teacher in the Indianapolis area for the last nine years, teaching in a 3- and 4-year-olds preschool for one year and kindergarten for the other eight. She has a bachelor's degree in elementary education, coupled with a kindergarten endorsement, as well as a master's degree in effective teaching and leadership, both from Butler University. Angle became aware of the principles and practices of Reggio Emilia during her time at Butler. Her long-standing interest in young children, fascination with emergent literacy, and experience with Reggio-inspired practices continue to guide her as a kindergarten teacher.

Karen K. Goldstein is a National Board Certified Teacher and a teacher consultant with the Hoosier Writing Project, an affiliate of the National Writing Project. She earned her bachelor's degree from Ball State University and her master's degree in effective teaching and leadership from Butler University. She has held many different positions during her career: preschool, kindergarten, third grade, and university teacher; IBM consultant; and instructional coach. Goldstein is currently working as an account manager for an educational publisher. Her love of reading and writing, along with her passionate belief in the young child's right to make sense of the world, drew her to study the ideas of Reggio Emilia and the structures of reading and writing workshop.

Alyssa Hildebrand is currently a kindergarten teacher at Adams Central Elementary in Monroe, Indiana. She began her teacher research journey while teaching kindergarten in the Indianapolis, Indiana, area, where she taught for seven years. Her educational career also includes serving as a transitional curriculum teacher, an EL coordinator, a high-ability coordinator, and a Title I teacher. She earned a master's degree from Butler University in effective teaching and leadership in 2007.

Patricia Durbin Horan is an instructional coach in a large metropolitan school district in Indianapolis, Indiana, where she presents professional development, collaborates with teachers to improve instructional practices, and helps to write curriculum. Before working as an instructional coach, she taught elementary school. She has a master's degree in effective teaching and leadership from Butler University and has enjoyed many years of teaching children and working with amazing professional educators.

Kristin Scibienski has been a kindergarten teacher in the Indianapolis, Indiana, area for the last eleven years and is currently working outside the classroom as a data interventionist, supporting elementary teachers and students as they navigate the link between data and instruction. She has a bachelor's degree in elementary education and a master's degree in effective teaching and leadership from Butler University. While at Butler, Scibienski was introduced to the principles of Reggio Emilia, and those understandings, coupled with her lifelong passion for reading and writing, have been foundational when creating classroom communities for young learners.

Jennifer Wheat has served in a variety of educational roles for the last eleven years, from teaching in the primary classroom and at the university level to serving as a district literacy specialist. In her current role as Title I coordinator, she leads instructional coaches in the district, collaborates with others to continuously improve the language arts curriculum, and provides professional development in a variety of areas related to literacy. Wheat has a bachelor's degree in elementary education and a master's degree in effective teaching and leadership from Butler University. She is currently pursuing her doctoral degree at Indiana University in the Department of Literacy, Culture, and Language Education. Throughout all of her experiences, Reggio fundamentals have provided the foundation for her thinking about teaching and learning.

This book was typeset in TheMix and Palatino by Barbara Frazier.

Typefaces used on the cover are Shannon Book and Bold, Garamond Book Condensed, and Gill Sans.

The book was printed on 50-lb. Opaque Offset paper by Versa Press, Inc.